THE CHILDREN'S EVERYDAY BIBLE

A BIBLE STORY FOR EVERY DAY OF THE YEAR

Illustrated by
ANNA C. LEPLAR

LONDON, NEW YORK, MUNICH,
MELBOURNE, AND DELHI

Project Editor Jane Chapman
Art Editor Jane Horne and Peter Bailey
Managing Editor Linda Esposito
Managing Art Editor Diane Thistlethwaite
DTP Designer Louise Paddick
Jacket Design Victoria Harvey
Production Shivani Pandey
Indexer Lynn Bresler
Religious consultant Penny Boshoff
U.S. Creative Director Jim Bolton
U.S. Project Editor Claudia Volkman
U.S. Editors Betty Free, Dave Barrett

Published in the United States by
Tyndale House Publishers, Inc.
351 Executive Drive, Carol Stream, IL 60188

ISBN 0-8423-6222-3

Colour reproduction by Colourscan, Singapore
Printed and bound in Singapore by Tien Wah Press
Visit Tyndale's exciting Web site at
www.tyndale.com

2 4 6 8 10 9 7 5 3 1

INTRODUCTION

The Children's Everyday Bible takes children on a fascinating journey to discover the people, places, and events of the Bible. With a new story for each day of the year, children will experience how God's love unfolds through the lives of different men and women. Each story stands on its own, so children can choose to read a day at a time or pick stories at random. Young children will enjoy flipping through the book, looking at the pictures, and selecting a story to be read to them. With older children, you may want to ask questions to help them apply the story to their own life. This is a book to be opened and enjoyed by the whole family throughout the year.

CONTENTS

CONTENTS

CONTENTS

CONTENTS

BIBLE LANDS

Rome

Puteoli

ITALY

BULGARIA

Philippi

PAUL AND
SILAS
IMPRISONED

Berea

Thessalonica

Troas

GREECE

SICILY

Athens

Ephesus

PAUL
SHIPWRECKED

Corinth

MALTA

CRETE

THE HOLY
LAND

Zarephath

JESUS FEEDS
THE CROWD

Mediterranean Sea

Capernaum

Cana

Nazareth

Sea of
Galilee

Shunem

Caesarea

MOSES IN THE
BULRUSHES

Samaria

EGYPT

Joppa

Shiloh

Lydda

N

Gibeon

Jericho

Emmaus

Jerusalem

Bethany

W

E

Bethlehem

THE BIRTH
OF JESUS

S

8

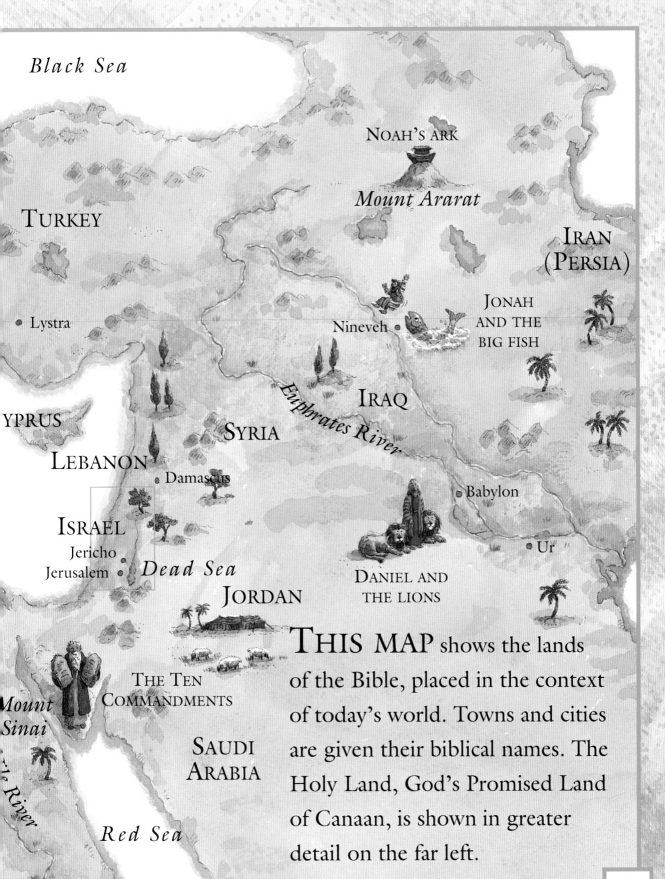

Black Sea

TURKEY

Lystra

CYPRUS

LEBANON

Damascus

ISRAEL

Jericho
Jerusalem

Dead Sea

Mount
Sinai

THE TEN
COMMANDMENTS

Red Sea

NOAH'S ARK

Mount Ararat

IRAN
(PERSIA)

Nineveh

JONAH
AND THE
BIG FISH

IRAQ

SYRIA

Euphrates River

Babylon

Ur

DANIEL AND
THE LIONS

JORDAN

SAUDI
ARABIA

THIS MAP shows the lands
of the Bible, placed in the context
of today's world. Towns and cities
are given their biblical names. The
Holy Land, God's Promised Land
of Canaan, is shown in greater
detail on the far left.

JANUARY 1

IN THE BEGINNING, God made the world, but it was very different from today's world. It was dark and empty. So God said, "Let there be light." God called the light "day" and the darkness "night." Next God made the sky, high above the earth. God made the rivers and seas and lakes and oceans, and he put dry land between them. God made all kinds of beautiful plants and trees to grow on the land. He made the bright sun to shine during the day, and he made the moon and lots of stars to shine at night. God saw that everything he made was good.

JANUARY 2

THE WORLD WAS BEAUTIFUL, but it was empty and quiet. So God made fish to swim in the seas, and birds to fly in the sky. He told the fish to make more fish, and the birds to make more birds. Then God made all kinds of animals, from tiny bugs to huge elephants and tall giraffes. Each animal was able to make more animals just like itself. Soon the world was full of living creatures. God was happy with everything that he had made so far.

JANUARY 3

THE MOST WONDERFUL part of God's new world was still to come. God made a man and called him Adam. God put Adam in charge of everything. So Adam wouldn't be lonely, God took a rib from Adam and made Eve. He placed them in a beautiful garden to live. And God was very pleased with his creation.

JANUARY 4

ADAM AND EVE WERE friends with God. They enjoyed everything that God had made. The garden where they lived was full of all kinds of amazing animals and birds, and beautiful trees and plants and flowers. There were many trees in the garden with good fruit to eat. But there was one tree that God did not want Adam and Eve to touch. "If you eat the fruit from that tree, you will die," God told them.

13

JANUARY 5

WHEN EVE WAS walking in the Garden of Eden one day, she saw a snake. The snake told Eve about the tree that God said not to touch. "If you eat the fruit from this tree," said the snake, "you will be wise like God." Eve wanted to be wise, and the fruit looked delicious. So Eve disobeyed God and took a bite of the fruit. Then she gave some to Adam, and he ate it too. When God saw what they did, he was both angry and sad. He told Adam and Eve to leave the garden.

JANUARY 6

ADAM AND EVE had two sons, Cain and Abel. Cain was a farmer and Abel was a shepherd. One day the brothers gave gifts to God. Cain gave some wheat from his fields, and Abel gave a young lamb. God was happy

with Abel's gift, but he didn't accept Cain's gift. This made Cain very angry. God said, "Why are you so angry? You will be accepted if you respond in the right way." Later Cain said to his brother, "Let's go out into the fields." While they were there, Cain killed Abel. Because of this, God sent Cain away. God told him he would have to wander from place to place for the rest of his life.

15

JANUARY 7

HUNDREDS OF YEARS after Adam and Eve, there were many people in God's world. But they didn't listen to God. No one thought good thoughts or did good things. God was sorry he had ever made people! He decided to send a flood to wash away everything. Only one man still loved and obeyed God. His name was Noah. God told Noah how to build a big boat called an ark. Then God told him to gather two of every kind of animal, one male and one female.

JANUARY 8

NOAH LISTENED to God. He built the ark and filled it with two of every kind of animal. Noah and his wife went into the ark too. His three sons and their wives went with them. There was just enough room for all of the people and animals. God closed the door and promised to keep them all safe.

JANUARY 9

DARK CLOUDS filled the sky, and it began to rain. But Noah, his family, and the animals were safe and dry in the ark. It rained for 40 days and 40 nights. Floodwaters soon covered the whole earth, but the ark floated on the water. When the rain stopped, the water slowly began to go down. The ark landed on a mountaintop. Noah sent out a dove several times. When it flew back with an olive branch in its beak, Noah knew the treetops were finally showing! God told Noah it was safe to leave the ark.

JANUARY 10

WHEN NOAH OPENED the door of the ark, the happy animals ran, jumped, crawled, and flew to freedom. Noah and his family were happy to be back on dry land too. They gave thanks to God for keeping them safe. God promised that he would never again send a flood to cover the whole earth. As a sign of this promise, God put a beautiful rainbow in the sky. It was the very first one!

19

JANUARY 11

ABRAHAM LIVED in a very nice house in the city of Ur. One day God surprised Abraham. God said, "Leave this city and go to a new country that I will show you. If you do this, I will bless you and make your family special." Abraham was 75 years old and it wasn't easy for him to get ready for a long trip. But he obeyed God and packed up all his things. He left home with his wife, Sarah, and his nephew, Lot. They weren't sure where they were going, or how long their journey would take.

JANUARY 12

ABRAHAM AND LOT had many sheep, cows, and goats. Both of them had servants who took care of their animals. These servants were always fighting over the best fields and water for the animals. Abraham wanted to stop these fights. "Let's live in different places," he said to Lot. "Then there will be plenty of grass for all our animals to eat." Abraham wanted to be kind, so he let Lot choose which place he wanted first. Lot chose the best place for himself, close to the river with lots of green grass. God was pleased that Abraham was kind to Lot. And God promised to give Abraham and his family lots of good land too.

JANUARY 13

IT DIDN'T SEEM POSSIBLE that Abraham and Sarah would ever have a child of their own. Sarah was 90, and Abraham was almost 100 years old. God wanted a whole nation of people to know and love him. So he made a special promise to Abraham and Sarah.

"Sarah will have a baby boy," said God. "You will call him Isaac. I will bless you with many, many children. And they will have many, many children. All of you will live in this beautiful country forever. But in return, I want you to promise you will always obey me."

JANUARY 14

ABRAHAM WAS SITTING by his tent when he saw three men walking towards him. It was a very hot day, so Abraham invited them to stop and rest in the shade. He gave them some cool water. "Stay and have something to eat too," he said. Abraham didn't know it, but one of the men was really God.

"Soon your wife will have a baby boy," this man said.

Sarah heard him and laughed. *I'm too old to have a child!* she thought. Because the man was God, he knew what she was thinking. "Nothing is impossible for God!" he told Sarah.

23

JANUARY 15

GOD KEPT HIS promise to Abraham and Sarah.

The next year Sarah gave birth to a baby boy, just like God said. Abraham named him Isaac, which means "he laughs." This was a good name because Isaac was a happy child, and he made his parents laugh. The name also reminded Sarah that she laughed because she did not believe God's promise to give her a son.

"Who would have thought that I would ever have a baby?" Sarah said. She thanked God for giving her Isaac.

JANUARY 16

ONE DAY God wanted to see how much Abraham loved him. God said, "Go up on a mountain. Give me your only son, Isaac, as a gift." Abraham trusted that God would take care of Isaac, who was now a young man. But since Abraham wanted to obey God, he climbed the mountain. He was ready to give his son back to God. Then God's angel stopped him and said, "Now I know that you love and obey God."

When Abraham saw a big sheep caught in a bush, he knew God had shown him the sheep. So he gave the sheep to God, and God was very pleased with Abraham's gift.

JANUARY 17

WHEN ISAAC grew up, Abraham wanted him to have a good wife. So Abraham said to one of his servants, "Go back to the country I left many years ago and find a wife for my son." After a long trip, the servant came to the town that Abraham was from. The servant stopped by a well and prayed to God, "Show me which woman you want to be Isaac's wife." When a beautiful young woman named Rebekah gave the servant and his camels water from the well, he knew that God had answered his prayer. Rebekah's family said she could go with the servant and marry Isaac.

JANUARY 18

ISAAC REMEMBERED

God's promise to his father about a big family. So he prayed for his wife, Rebekah, to have a child. Before long, Isaac and Rebekah became the parents of twin boys named Esau and Jacob. When the two boys grew up, Esau loved to be outdoors and hunt wild deer. That made his father happy. Jacob liked to stay close to home. That made his mother happy. Esau was born just a few minutes before Jacob, so he would be the head of the family someday. But one day Esau was very hungry. His brother had just made stew. So, for a bowl of stew, Esau gave Jacob the right to be head of the family.

27

JANUARY 19

WHEN ISAAC grew old, he was almost blind. He wanted to give a special family blessing to his older son, Esau. "Go out hunting and kill a deer," he said to Esau. "Then fix the meat the way I like it, and I will bless you."

Rebekah told Jacob, their younger son, "I'll fix some meat that *you* can give to your father." Then she covered Jacob's arms with goat hair so they would feel like Esau's. When Jacob took the food to Isaac, the old man touched him. "You sound like Jacob but feel like Esau," said Isaac. Then he gave Jacob his blessing.

28

JANUARY 20

SOON ESAU CAME BACK

from his hunting trip. He fixed some meat and took it into Isaac's tent. Right away, both Isaac and Esau knew that Jacob had tricked them. Esau was very angry. "Someday I will kill my brother!" he shouted. Rebekah heard about Esau's plan. She knew she had to act quickly to save her younger son, Jacob.

"Let's send Jacob to live with my family," Rebekah told Isaac, and he agreed. So Jacob packed up all his things and said good-bye to his parents. He was sad to leave home, but he knew he had to escape from his angry brother.

29

JANUARY 21

JACOB FELT LONELY as he started on his trip. When the sun set at the end of the first day, he lay down on the ground to sleep. He put a stone under his head for a pillow. Jacob dreamed of a wide stairway reaching up into heaven, with angels going up and down it. He saw God at the top of the stairway. "I am the God of Abraham and Isaac," God said to Jacob. "I am also your God, and I will keep my promise to give you a big family. Wherever you go, I will take care of you."

Jacob woke up full of wonder. "Please bring me home safely, God," prayed Jacob. "And I will always obey you."

JANUARY 22

AFTER HIS dream, Jacob was ready to travel again. He hurried on his way and finally came to his mother's hometown. Jacob asked some shepherds standing by a well if they knew Laban, his uncle.

"Yes, we do," they said. "Look, here comes Laban's daughter, Rachel." Jacob turned and saw a beautiful woman walking toward him. She was leading her father's sheep to the well so she could give them some water. Jacob told Rachel who he was. She ran right home to tell her father, Laban, about meeting Jacob. Laban went to see Jacob and welcome him to his home.

JANUARY 23

JACOB BEGAN WORKING for his uncle.

"How should I pay you?" Laban asked.

"I'll work for you for seven years and then marry your daughter Rachel," Jacob said. The years flew by quickly for Jacob because he loved Rachel so much. On the night of the wedding, Laban brought his daughter to Jacob. But the next morning, Jacob saw that Laban had tricked him. Laban had brought Jacob his oldest daughter, Leah, instead of Rachel! Jacob was angry, but Laban said that Leah was the older sister, so she should be married first. Laban told Jacob he could marry Rachel too if he worked another seven years.

So Jacob did!

JANUARY 24

JACOB AND LABAN did not always get along. But Jacob still worked hard for his uncle. After 20 years, Jacob knew it was time to go back home. Laban promised Jacob he could have more sheep if he would stay. But Laban did not keep his promise. God told Jacob to leave, so he left in a hurry with his family. It was a big family now. Laban followed them. He wanted to say good-bye to his daughters and his grandchildren. After this, Jacob and Laban parted peacefully.

JANUARY 25

ON THE TRIP back home, Jacob could not stop thinking about Esau, his brother. Many years ago, Jacob had played a mean trick on Esau. Now Jacob wondered if his twin brother was still angry. He wondered if Esau still wanted to kill him. Jacob sent his family and all his animals on ahead, but he stayed behind to think alone. That night, he prayed that God would not let him or his family be hurt. Then, out of nowhere, a strange man came to fight with Jacob.

"People will call you Israel," said the man as they were fighting together. "This means you struggled with God and people." After a long fight, the man left. He did not say what his name was, but Jacob knew he had met God that night.

JANUARY 26

EARLY THE NEXT MORNING, Jacob caught up with the rest of his family. Suddenly in the distance, he saw Esau and a big crowd of men coming toward them. Jacob was afraid for his big family and also for himself. But he knew he had to be brave and go ahead of his family. Jacob walked slowly toward his brother. What a happy surprise it was when Esau ran up to him and hugged him! Then Jacob knew that Esau was no longer angry with him. The brothers both cried happy tears when they saw each other again.

JANUARY 27

JACOB HAD 12 SONS, but his favorite was Joseph. Because Jacob loved him so much, he gave his son a colorful coat. Joseph showed the coat to his brothers. Then he told them about a strange dream he had.

"We were in the fields tying up bundles of corn. My bundle stood up straight, and yours bowed down to mine," said Joseph. This made his brothers angry.

"Do you really think you can rule over us?" they asked.

Joseph went on, "In another dream, the sun, moon, and 11 stars all bowed down to me." Then his brothers hated Joseph more than ever.

JANUARY 28

ONE DAY Joseph was at home with his father. His brothers were out in the fields, looking after their father's sheep. Jacob was worried because his older sons had been away for a long time. "Go and see if your brothers are safe," he said to Joseph. The brothers saw Joseph when he was still far away because he was easy to spot in his long, colorful coat. They were so angry with him that they wanted to kill him. But Reuben, the oldest, talked his brothers into throwing Joseph into a deep pit instead.

JANUARY 29

SOME TRADERS PASSED by on their way to
Egypt to sell their spices. This gave one brother, Judah, an
idea. "Let's sell Joseph as a slave. That way we can get rid
of him and earn some money at the same time," he said.
So they pulled Joseph out of the pit, took his coat, and
sold him to the traders. Then they dipped his beautiful
coat in goat's blood and brought it home to their father.

"A wild animal must have killed my dear son!" cried
the old man. He was very sad, and no one could make
him feel better.

JANUARY 30

JOSEPH WAS NOT DEAD, as his father thought, but alive and well in Egypt. He was bought as a slave by Potiphar, an officer at the palace. Joseph always worked hard, so Potiphar put him in charge of his house. Everyone liked Joseph, especially Potiphar's wife. One day she tried to kiss him, but Joseph pushed her away because he knew it was wrong to kiss someone else's wife. This made her angry, so she lied to her husband. She said that Joseph had tried to kiss *her*. Potiphar was very upset, so he had Joseph thrown into jail.

JANUARY 31

TWO OTHER MEN were put in jail with Joseph. One was the king's baker, and the other was the

waiter who served wine to the king. One night both men had dreams. The waiter dreamed of a vine with three branches filled with grapes. He squeezed grape juice into the king's cup. Joseph told the waiter, "In three days the king will give you back your job. When he does, please ask him to set me free."

The baker dreamed he was carrying three baskets of cakes to the king, but birds came and ate all of them. Joseph told him, "The king will sentence you to die in three days." And it all happened just as Joseph said!

FEBRUARY 1

THE WAITER

forgot all about asking the king to let Joseph out of jail. Two years passed and then the king had two dreams that no one could understand.

Suddenly the waiter remembered Joseph. "I know someone who can help," he said. So Joseph was brought to the king. "In my first dream, seven thin cows ate up seven fat cows," said the king. "In the second dream, seven thin stalks of grain ate up seven full stalks."

Joseph explained, "God is telling you there will be seven years of good crops. But those years will be followed by seven years of bad crops, and during this time there will be no food to eat."

41

FEBRUARY 2

JOSEPH TOLD THE KING of Egypt, "When the crops of grain in the fields grow well, store some of the grain away. Then everyone will have grain during the seven years when the crops stop growing."

The king said to Joseph, "You are a wise man. I will put you in charge. I will be the only person in Egypt who is more important than you."

So, for the next seven years, Joseph stored much of the grain. Then the crops stopped growing. But because Joseph stored some of the grain, everyone had enough food to eat.

FEBRUARY 3

JOSEPH'S FAMILY didn't have enough to eat, so his 10 older brothers came to Egypt to buy food. They did not recognize Joseph, but he knew who they were. He wanted to see if they had changed. "You're spies," he said.

"No, we're not!" They told Joseph about their father and their younger brother, Benjamin, waiting at home.

"Bring your little brother to me so I will know that your story is true," said Joseph. "I'll keep one of you with me here in Egypt until the rest of you come back."

43

FEBRUARY 4

JACOB DIDN'T want Benjamin to go to Egypt with his brothers. But when they ran out of food again, Jacob finally let Benjamin go. Joseph gave his brothers dinner at the palace. But he still didn't tell them who he was. Soon they left for home with big bags of grain. They didn't know that Joseph had hidden his silver cup in Benjamin's bag. Joseph's servant ran after the brothers. He asked, "Who stole my master's silver cup?" Then he found the cup in Benjamin's bag. Worried and scared, the brothers returned to face Joseph. Judah said to Joseph, "Keep me here as your slave, but please let Benjamin go back to his father."

Now Joseph knew his brothers had really changed. "I am Joseph, your long-lost brother!" he told them.

FEBRUARY 5

JOSEPH'S BROTHERS were afraid. They knew how badly they had treated Joseph before. But Joseph told them not to worry. "It was God's plan that I should come to Egypt," he said. "Just go home and bring my father back with you." Their father, Jacob, could hardly believe the wonderful news! He and his sons and their families packed their things and set off for Egypt. Joseph rode out to greet everyone. He gave his father a big hug. They were happy to be together again.

February 6

Egypt had a new king. Joseph and his brothers were no longer living, but their children and grandchildren kept having more children. The king was worried because there were so many of God's people living in his country. He thought they might fight against the people of Egypt. So the king was very mean to them. He forced God's people to work for him as slaves. But no matter how hard he made them work, there were more and more of God's people every day. So many babies were born that the king didn't know what to do. Finally he ordered, "Throw all of the new baby boys in the Nile River!"

FEBRUARY 7

ONE WOMAN WANTED to be sure her baby boy would be safe. So she made a basket that would float on the water. She hid her baby inside and carefully placed the basket in the Nile River. The baby's sister, Miriam, watched from a distance. When the king's daughter came to bathe in the river, she found the basket. Miriam ran up to the princess and said, "Let me find a nurse to look after this baby for you." Miriam went to get her mother, who cared for the baby until he was old enough to live at the palace. The princess named him Moses.

FEBRUARY 8

MOSES GREW UP in the palace, but he never felt like an Egyptian prince. He watched God's people, the Israelites, working hard as slaves for their mean Egyptian masters, and he felt sad. He knew that he was one of God's people, even though he was treated like a prince.

One day Moses saw an Egyptian man beating a slave. This made Moses so angry that he killed the Egyptian man and hid his body in the sand. When the king heard what Moses had done, he was very upset. He even tried to kill Moses. So Moses ran far away to another country.

FEBRUARY 9

ONE DAY MOSES WAS SITTING alone by a well. Seven sisters came to the well and began to fill their big jars with water for their father's sheep. Then some other shepherds came to the well and tried to push the sisters out of the way. Moses helped the women and made sure they got all the water they needed. The sisters and their father, Jethro, were very thankful and asked Moses to come to their house for dinner. Soon the family invited Moses to stay and live with them. Moses married one of the sisters, Zipporah, and they had a baby boy.

FEBRUARY 10

MOSES WORKED AS a shepherd, taking care of the sheep that belonged to his wife's father. One day Moses took the sheep close to Mount Sinai, where there was good grass for them to eat. He looked up and saw a strange sight. A bush was on fire, but it did not seem to be burning up in the flames. Suddenly God spoke to Moses from the bush. God said that he had seen how unhappy his people were in Egypt. "I'm going to save my people from the cruel Egyptians," said God. "I want you, Moses, to lead them out of Egypt and take them to a beautiful new land."

FEBRUARY 11

MOSES WAS SURPRISED that God would choose him to lead his people out of Egypt. "How can I lead your people?" he asked God. "I'm not special. No one will ever follow me anywhere!" God promised to help Moses, but Moses still didn't think he could do it. So God told Moses that his brother, Aaron, could help him. The two of them could work as a team. God would give Moses the power to do miracles, and he would give Aaron the right words to say to the people. So Moses obeyed God and made plans to go back to Egypt.

FEBRUARY 12

WHEN MOSES AND AARON arrived in Egypt, they met with the leaders of God's people. Aaron

told them about God's promise to take his people to a land where they would be free. The leaders were glad to hear this news and thanked God for it. Then Moses and Aaron went to see the king. They asked him to let God's people leave Egypt. They told the king that God said, "Let my people go!"

The king became very angry. "Your people are just lazy," he shouted. "Now I will make them work even harder. I will not let them go." So God's people were more unhappy than before, and they were upset with Moses.

FEBRUARY 13

GOD TOLD MOSES he had not forgotten his promise to free his people. But when Moses and Aaron went back to the palace, the king still would not let God's people go. God turned the waters of the Nile River red with blood, but this did not change the king's mind. Each time the king refused to listen, God sent new troubles to the people of Egypt. Their homes were filled with frogs and huge swarms of flies. Their animals died, and the Egyptian people themselves broke out in sore spots. Big hailstones fell from the sky and killed all their crops. But the king still wouldn't let God's people leave Egypt.

53

FEBRUARY 14

NEXT GOD SENT an army of
hungry locusts to gobble the Egyptians'
plants and trees. Then he made it completely
dark for three whole days. God kept his own
people safe from all these troubles. But the
king still would not let God's people leave Egypt.
Moses and Aaron went to see the king one last time. "God
will now send the most terrible trouble he has ever sent to
your people," warned Moses. "After this, you will let
us go. At midnight, the oldest son in every
Egyptian home will die. There will be
sadness everywhere."

FEBRUARY 15

GOD PROMISED TO KEEP his people safe from this last horrible thing he was sending to the Egyptians. Moses told the people what to do so the angel of death would pass over their homes. Each father had to paint the blood from his best lamb or goat around the doors of his house. In the evening the whole family ate a special meal. Late that night the oldest son in every Egyptian family died. But in each home of God's people, the oldest son was safe. That's because God's people had obeyed and trusted him.

55

FEBRUARY 16

FINALLY THE KING SAID God's people could go! So that night, Moses led God's people out of Egypt. But the king soon began to miss them. Who would do the hard work now that his slaves were gone? So the king sent his soldiers after God's people to bring them back to Egypt. The soldiers caught up with them as they were camping by the Red Sea. God's people were trapped! But Moses told them not to be afraid, because God had promised to protect them.

FEBRUARY 17

GOD TOLD MOSES TO HOLD his big wooden stick over the Red Sea. The people were surprised when God made the wind blow the waves apart so there was a dry path between the waters. Moses led the people to the other side. When the Egyptian soldiers tried to follow them, the wheels of their chariots got

stuck in the wet sand. The waves crashed back over the path before the army could get across. God kept his people safe as they traveled on. During the day, there was always a tall cloud just ahead of them. And every night there was a pillar of fire that showed them the way.

FEBRUARY 18

ALL THE PEOPLE sang a happy song to God. They thanked him for parting the water in the Red Sea so they could get away from Egypt. Then Moses led God's people into the desert. They walked for three long days without finding any water. At last they found water, but it tasted horrible. The people were upset with Moses. So God showed Moses a tree branch and told him to throw it into the water. After Moses did that, the water was good to drink. God reminded his people that if they obeyed him, he would take care of them.

FEBRUARY 19

THE DESERT WAS HOT and God's people were tired and hungry. They complained to Moses, "We were better off in Egypt. Here we will starve!" Moses didn't know what to do, but he asked God for help. God told Moses he would supply all the food they needed. That evening a large flock of quails covered the ground, and everyone had plenty of meat to eat. The next morning the ground was covered with strange white flakes. They tasted sweet, like bread with honey. The people were puzzled and asked, "What is it?" Moses told them it was the food God had promised. The people called this special food "manna." Everyone ate manna for the rest of their long trip.

FEBRUARY 20

GOD'S PEOPLE complained a lot as they traveled. They found it hard to believe that God would take care of them. One day they stopped to rest, but there was no water for them to drink. Everyone was hot, thirsty, and very grumpy. "Why did you bring us here, Moses?" the people asked. Some were so angry that they picked up stones to throw at their leader. God told Moses to take his special stick and hit a rock with it. When Moses did that, an amazing thing happened! Water began to flow out from the rock. Now there was water for everyone!

FEBRUARY 21

ONE DAY JETHRO, MOSES' father-in-law, came to visit Moses in the desert. Moses told Jethro about all the wonderful things God had done for his people. Jethro thanked God for his great goodness. Jethro saw how much time Moses spent settling arguments between people who weren't getting along. Jethro told Moses, "You need helpers to share this huge job with you or you will wear yourself out!" Moses listened to Jethro. He chose a group of honest men to work with him. Together they taught the people how to please God and get along with each other.

FEBRUARY 22

MOSES CLIMBED Mount Sinai to pray. God told Moses, "Remind the people how I rescued them and cared for them so far on this journey. If they will obey me, they will always be my own special people." Two days later everyone gathered at the bottom of the mountain. There was a loud trumpet blast, and suddenly the top of the mountain was full of smoke and fire! The people were afraid because they knew God was on top of the mountain. Moses climbed the mountain again to talk with God. When God answered, the people below heard loud thunder. But it was really God talking!

FEBRUARY 23

GOD GAVE MOSES ten

special laws, called the Ten
Commandments. These laws
told the people how to act. The
people were to worship only God
and not make idols of gods that aren't
real. They were to use his name with care.
They were to rest on God's day each
week, and children were to obey their
parents. Killing another person was
against God's law. So was stealing
another person's wife or husband,
or anything else that belonged to
them. No one was to tell lies
or want to have other
people's things. If the
people obeyed these
laws, they would live
happily together.

FEBRUARY 24

MOSES SPENT many days talking to God at the top of Mount Sinai. He was gone so long that the people became impatient. "Make a god to lead us," they begged Aaron. So Aaron told the crowd to bring him their gold. They did, and Aaron made an idol that looked like a calf. Everyone worshiped the idol and had a wild party. Then Moses came down the mountain carrying two big, flat stones with God's commandments written on them. When he saw the golden calf, he was so angry that he dropped the big stones. They smashed into tiny pieces!

FEBRUARY 25

MOSES WAS VERY UPSET with Aaron and with all the people who had worshiped the golden calf. "But I'll ask God to forgive you," he said. So once again, Moses met with God on Mount Sinai. At first God was angry. But because God loved his people, he forgave them. He promised that he would continue to be with them on their journey. Then, on two more big, flat stones, God again wrote his Ten Commandments for Moses to take to the people.

FEBRUARY 26

GOD'S PEOPLE kept moving, so they couldn't put up a building in one place to worship God. But they still needed somewhere special to go to pray. "Make a big tent," God told Moses. "It will be a special place for you to talk to me. Use all the best materials.

Everybody who wants to can bring gifts to help with the work. When the tent is finished, you can take it with you on your journey." God's people made this tent, called the tabernacle, as beautiful as possible. They gave fine cloth, animal skins, gold, silver, and many other wonderful gifts. Finally, Moses told the people to stop. He had more than enough to make God's tent!

FEBRUARY 27

AT LAST the Israelites had almost reached the land God promised them. So Moses chose 12 men to learn all about this Promised Land. There was one man from each of the 12 groups, or tribes. These men, who were gone for six weeks, came back with many kinds of fruit. But the news they brought back was not good. "This beautiful land will never be ours," they said. "The people are like huge giants, so how can we take over their cities?"

FEBRUARY 28

ONCE AGAIN God's people began to complain bitterly. "Why did we ever leave Egypt?" they grumbled. Caleb, one of the 12 spies, said, "We must trust God to give us the land he promised us. Let's go!" His friend Joshua agreed with him. "God will help us!" The people wouldn't listen. They even wanted to kill Joshua and Caleb. This made God very angry. He told Moses, "My people must wander in the desert for 40 years. They will never see the land of Canaan, but their children will enter the land. And Joshua and Caleb will be their leaders."

FEBRUARY 29

GOD NEVER LEFT his people
during their long trip through the desert.
Many times the people made God sad and
angry. But there was never a single moment
when God stopped caring for them. As they
moved from place to place, God made sure
his people had food, water, clothes, and a
place to sleep. More than anything, God wanted his people
to know that he was their God. He made a special promise,
called a covenant. He promised he would always
look after his people, just as he had done before.
In return, he wanted the people to make a
promise too. Their part of the
covenant was to love and
obey him.

MARCH 1

MOSES LIVED TO BE a very old man. He knew that a younger leader would have to take his people into the Promised Land.

Moses talked to Joshua, his helper. "God wants you to lead his people now. You must trust God to help you. Do not be afraid, because God will always be with you."

Then Moses said to the people, "It is time for you to enter the country that belongs to you. God will go ahead of you and will get rid of your enemies. Then their land will belong to you. Joshua is your new leader, and he will go with you, just as God promised. Be brave and remember that God is with you. He will never leave you."

MARCH 2

MOSES WAS SAD that he would never be able to enter the Promised Land. But God told Moses to climb high up on a mountain called Mount Nebo. There Moses could see the whole land of Canaan that was soon going to belong to God's people. Moses died in the land of Moab without entering the Promised Land. He was 120 years old! After Moses died, Joshua took over the job of leading God's people. He was full of God's wisdom. So right from the start the people listened to Joshua.

MARCH 3

GOD TALKED TO JOSHUA, the new leader of God's people. "Get ready to go across the Jordan River into the land of Canaan," God said. "I will give you the whole country, and no one will be able to stand up to you or stop you. I will always be with you, just as I was with Moses. Do not be afraid. If you obey me, everything will always go well for you."

Joshua told the people to get ready to enter the Promised Land in just three days. The people were excited. They said, "We'll do whatever you ask. We'll go wherever you send us."

MARCH 4

THREE TRIBES OF God's people lived on the east side of the Jordan River. The Promised Land was on the west side of the river. Joshua reminded the  three tribes what God wanted them to do. Their wives and children could stay on the east side of the river, but all the men were to go across with the other tribes to win the land of Canaan. Later, when the fighting was over, these brave men could return to live with their families and tend their herds in the rich pastures on the east side of the river.

MARCH 5

BEFORE GOD'S PEOPLE could get to Canaan, they had to go through the city of Jericho. This city had a big wall all around it. So Joshua sent two spies to Jericho to find out all they could. The spies came to Rahab's house. She was kind and hid the men on her roof to keep them safe. A little while later, some of the king's men knocked on Rahab's door, looking for the spies. But Rahab told the king's men that her visitors had already left the city. So the men went away to hunt for the spies. They didn't see the spies hiding on Rahab's roof!

MARCH 6

RAHAB WENT UP on her roof to talk with the two spies. "I know God will give my country to your people," said Rahab. "Since I have helped you, please be kind to me and my family. When your people take over this city, please keep us safe." The spies promised to do that. Then Rahab let down a red rope that was tied to her window so the spies could escape. The men told Rahab to leave the red rope hanging from her window. They said, "This will show our people where your family is hiding, so we can keep all of you safe." Then the men climbed down the rope and left.

MARCH 7

THE TWO SPIES went back to the other side of the Jordan River. "We're sure God will give us this whole land!" they told Joshua. So the people got ready to cross the river. The water was deep, but Joshua sent the priests ahead of the people. They carried a special box called the ark of the covenant that contained God's laws. When the priests stepped into the river, the water stopped flowing and there was a dry path! The priests stayed there until God's people were all safely on the other side.

MARCH 8

GOD TOLD JOSHUA to have one man from each of the 12 tribes take a stone from the dry path in the river. Then priests walked across to the other side of the river, and the water started to flow again. Now God's people knew that Joshua was a good leader, just as Moses had been. The 12 men placed their 12 stones together in a tall pile. "Your children will grow up someday and look at these stones. And they will remember how God brought us all safely across the Jordan River and into the Promised Land," said Joshua.

MARCH 9

JOSHUA STOOD LOOKING at the city of Jericho, with its tall, scary walls. Suddenly a man walked up to him, holding a sword. "Are you a friend or an enemy?" asked Joshua.

"I am in charge of God's army," answered the man.

Then Joshua knew that this was not just any man. He was a very special messenger sent by God. Joshua also knew that all he had to do was listen to God's messenger and obey his commands. Then the city of Jericho would belong to God's people. Joshua told the man, "I will do whatever you tell me to do."

MARCH 10

GOD TOLD JOSHUA to have the people march around Jericho. Soldiers went first, followed by priests who played trumpets. Behind them were priests carrying the ark of the covenant. More soldiers came next, followed by the rest of the people. The group marched around Jericho once a day for six days, with trumpets blowing. On the seventh day they went around the city seven times, giving a loud shout the last time. As the people shouted, the city walls crashed to the ground! The soldiers set the city on fire, but they saved Rahab and her family as the spies had promised.

79

MARCH 11

THE CANAANITES were afraid when they saw what happened to Jericho. Some Canaanites from Gibeon tried to trick Joshua. They went to see him, dressed in old clothes. "We've come from far away," they said. "Let's be friends." Joshua agreed because he didn't know they were really his enemies. When he found out they had lied to him, he was angry. Since he had already promised not to fight them, he forced them to become slaves. From then on, the Gibeonites had to cut wood and carry water for God's people.

MARCH 12

AFTER MANY LONG BATTLES with their enemies, God's people were ready to live in peace. They planned to live in the land of Canaan. But first everyone gathered at Shiloh. There they put up the tabernacle where they worshiped God. Now their special tent could stay in one place.

While Joshua was at Shiloh, God helped him to be fair and give land to each of the Israelite tribes. Joshua told each tribe that the land was a generous gift from God.

MARCH 13

WHEN JOSHUA DIVIDED the land, one tribe, the Levites, did not get its share because God had chosen them for a special purpose. He wanted them to be his holy priests. God knew they would not have time for his work if they had to farm the land. So Joshua told the other 11 tribes to give some of their fields and cities to the Levites. This way, the Levites had enough land to live on. And they were able to spend all their time praying to God and helping God's people worship him.

MARCH 14

WHEN THE LAND was divided up, Joshua called God's people together. "Long ago God promised to give this land to Abraham, and he promised Abraham a big family. You are all part of Abraham's big family! Now you have come to live in this beautiful land, and you must promise to obey God." Right away the people agreed. Joshua rolled a big stone beneath the oak tree beside the tabernacle of the Lord. He did this to help the people remember their promise to obey God.

MARCH 15

JOSHUA LED GOD'S PEOPLE until the day he died. Without a new leader to guide them, no one seemed to remember any of the great things God had done. They disobeyed God and began to worship idols again. All this made God very sad and very angry. He sent an enemy army to defeat the Israelites and make them slaves. The people told God they were sorry and begged him for help. God never stopped loving his people, so he gave them a new leader called a judge to help them do the right thing.

MARCH 16

BECAUSE GOD'S people turned away from him again, God let King Eglon of Moab rule over them for many years. King Eglon made God's people so miserable that they finally asked God for help. God still loved his people. So he chose Ehud to be a judge and help his people. One day, Ehud went to see King Eglon, hiding a sharp sword in his clothes. When the two men were alone, Ehud pulled out the sword and killed the king. He left the palace without being seen. Later, Ehud's army defeated the people of Moab. The Israelites were free again!

MARCH 17

GOD'S PEOPLE LIVED in peace for 80 years after Ehud won his fight with the people of Moab. But then Ehud died, and the people forgot about God again. So God allowed a cruel Canaanite king named Jabin to rule over the people. After 20 years of being treated badly, the people again begged God for help. A wise woman named Deborah was now their judge. She sent for Barak, an army general. Together they would help God's people win another amazing battle.

MARCH 18

DEBORAH TOLD BARAK to gather 10,000 soldiers to fight Sisera, the leader of King Jabin's army. Sisera had 900 iron chariots and a huge army. Barak asked Deborah to go with him into battle. God told Deborah the right time to attack the enemy army. When she gave the order, Barak's army charged down a hillside. They surprised their enemies and won the fight! But Sisera escaped by hiding in a tent that belonged to a woman named Jael. He thought he was safe, but when he fell asleep, Jael killed him with a sharp tent peg. With Sisera dead, Barak's army completely defeated King Jabin and his people.

MARCH 19

FORTY YEARS passed peacefully. But when the Israelites began to disobey God again, new enemies, the Midianites, appeared. These people stole all the Israelites' crops and animals and left nothing to eat! After seven miserable years, the people begged God for help. So God chose Gideon, a farmer. Gideon wasn't sure he could do such a big job. "I'm no hero!" he told God. But God said, "I will make you strong."

MARCH 20

GIDEON WANTED TO be sure God had chosen him to lead the battle against the Midianites. So he asked God for a sign. Gideon put some sheep's wool on the ground. "If this wool is wet with dew in the morning but the ground is dry, I'll know you've chosen me," he told God. The next day the ground was dry. But the wool was so wet that Gideon squeezed out a whole bowl full of water. Still he asked God for *another* sign. "Tomorrow, if the wool stays dry while the ground is wet with dew, I'll know for sure!" The next morning, the ground sparkled with dew, but the wool was fluffy and dry. Finally Gideon believed that God had chosen him to rescue the Israelites.

89

MARCH 21

GIDEON'S ARMY WAS very big. "The people will think they won because they were so strong," God told Gideon. "Trust me to help you win." So Gideon did what God told him. He sent all but 300 soldiers home. Late one night these men went to the enemy camp. They blew trumpets and smashed clay jars with blazing torches hidden inside. Then they shouted loudly and held up their torches. The noise and light scared the sleeping Midianites so much that they ran away! The battle was won!

MARCH 22

BECAUSE GOD'S PEOPLE forgot their promise to obey God again, new enemies called the Philistines began to rule over them. But a man named Manoah and his wife trusted God. One day an angel told Manoah's wife that she would have a baby boy who would grow up to lead the fight against the Philistines. This was a great surprise, for both Manoah and his wife were very old. A while later their baby was born, and they named him Samson. He never had a haircut to show he had been set apart to serve God.

MARCH 23

SAMSON GREW UP to be very, very strong. He was also very stubborn and did whatever he wanted. When Samson wanted to marry a Philistine woman, his parents were upset. The Philistines didn't believe in God. But Samson married her anyway. Later Samson left his wife and went back home to live with his parents. Then he fell in love with Delilah, another Philistine woman. She was beautiful, but Samson shouldn't have trusted her. The Philistines asked Delilah to find out what made Samson so strong. She finally learned the truth—it was Samson's long hair that gave him his strength. Delilah quickly told her friends Samson's secret. Then she hid these enemies of Samson's in her house. When Samson went to sleep, Delilah let them cut off his hair. And when Samson woke up, both his hair and his strength were gone!

MARCH 24

THE PHILISTINES captured Samson and threw him in prison. They blinded him and put him in bronze chains. They had a big party to celebrate their victory. But Samson's hair had begun growing. He prayed to God for strength again. "Let me die with the Philistines!" he shouted. Then he pushed as hard as he could against the pillars he was standing between. The whole building crashed to the ground! Samson and the Philistines were killed.

MARCH 25

NAOMI LIVED in Bethlehem with her husband and two sons. One year no crops grew in the fields, and nobody had any food. So the whole family moved to the country of Moab, where there was plenty to eat. Not long after that, Naomi's husband died. Her two sons married young women from Moab. Then both of Naomi's sons also died. Now she was all alone. The young women who had married her sons were named Ruth and Orpah. They did their best to help their mother-in-law feel better. But Naomi was homesick for her own country. So she decided to leave Moab and go back home.

MARCH 26

RUTH AND ORPAH WANTED to travel with Naomi. So the three women began their trip back to Bethlehem. Naomi loved Ruth and Orpah, but she didn't want to take them so far away from their home. She told them to return to their parents so they could remarry while they were still young.

Orpah sadly kissed Naomi and said good-bye. But Ruth wouldn't leave. "Let me stay!" she said. "Wherever you go, I will go!"

Naomi agreed, and together they traveled to Naomi's hometown of Bethlehem.

MARCH 27

IN BIBLE TIMES women couldn't earn money to buy food. So Ruth went out to gather the grain that was left over in one of the fields. At least she and Naomi could make bread from the grain. As Ruth was working, Boaz, the owner of the field, saw her. He had heard how much Ruth loved her mother-in-law. So he wanted to do something kind for Ruth. "If you are thirsty, drink the water from the jars in the fields," he told her. Then he told his workers to leave extra grain in the fields. Boaz wanted to be sure there was plenty of grain for Ruth to pick up and take home.

MARCH 28

NAOMI WAS SURPRISED

when Ruth came home with a basket full of grain and told her about Boaz. "God is good to us!" she said. "Boaz is one of my relatives!" So Ruth kept working in Boaz's fields as long as there was grain.

Then Naomi had a plan. "Find Boaz when he is alone," she told Ruth. "Ask him to help us because we are family." Ruth did as she was told.

Boaz said he would buy the land that at one time had belonged to Naomi's husband. Then he married Ruth and let Naomi live in their home. Naomi was very happy when Ruth and Boaz had a baby boy. Naomi was no longer alone!

MARCH 29

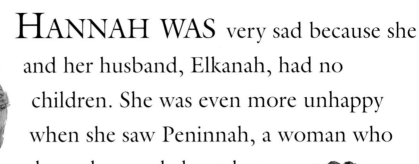

HANNAH WAS very sad because she and her husband, Elkanah, had no children. She was even more unhappy when she saw Peninnah, a woman who always bragged about her big family. And she made fun of Hannah for not having any children. Once a year, Elkanah took his family to worship God at Shiloh.

That's where the tabernacle was. While Hannah was there, she felt very alone and very sad. She went to the tent to pray. Tears rolled down her cheeks as she talked to God. "If you give me a child," she cried, "I promise I will give him back to you. And he will serve you all his life."

MARCH 30

ELI, THE PRIEST who lived at the tabernacle, heard Hannah crying. He asked her what was wrong.

"I'm very upset because I have no children!" Hannah told him. "And I've been asking God for help."

"May God answer your prayers," Eli said kindly.

Hannah went back home. Soon she learned she was going to have a baby! When her son Samuel was born, Hannah didn't forget her promise. Samuel was still a child when Hannah brought him to Shiloh. He became Eli's helper in the tent.

99

March 31

Eli and Samuel spent all their time at the tabernacle. They even slept there. One night Samuel heard someone calling his name. Thinking Eli needed him, Samuel went to him. "Here I am!" he said.

"I didn't ask for you," said Eli. "Go back to bed." The same thing happened two more times. By the third time, Eli knew God was calling Samuel. "Listen to what God is saying to you," Eli told the boy. After that night, God spoke to Samuel many times. The boy grew up to be a great prophet who told the Israelites what God said.

APRIL 1

THE PHILISTINES grew stronger and began fighting with God's people again. So the leaders of Israel came up with an idea. "Let's take the ark of the covenant to war with us," they said. "Then we will win!" But nobody asked God's advice about this plan! And when the Philistine soldiers saw the ark, they fought even harder. Over 30,000 of Israel's soldiers died—including Eli's two sons. The rest of God's people ran back to their tents. The Philistines grabbed the ark and took it away with them.

APRIL 2

THE PHILISTINES WERE pleased to have captured the ark with God's laws in it. They placed it next to a huge idol in their temple. The next morning the Philistines found their idol facedown on the ground in front of the ark. They carefully picked it up. But that night it fell again with a loud crash and broke into pieces. Now the Philistines were afraid! So they sent the ark back to God's people, who were glad to see it again.

APRIL 3

SAMUEL WAS WISE and he ruled Israel for many years. But when Samuel grew old, the people began to think about what kind of leader they wanted next. "We want a king," they told Samuel. "All of the other countries have kings!"

This upset Samuel. He thought the people didn't like him as a leader. But God told Samuel what the real reason was. The people didn't want to be ruled by God anymore.

"Let my people have their way, " God said to Samuel. "But tell them that a king may not treat them the way they think he should."

APRIL 4

SAUL WAS THE SON of a farmer named Kish. Saul was a tall, good-looking young man, and he often helped his father. One day Saul's father sent him out to look for some lost donkeys. After searching for three days, Saul began to give up hope of ever finding the animals.

"Let's go home before my father begins to worry," Saul told his servant. "He'll worry more about us than the donkeys!"

But the servant said, "I have an idea. We're not far from where Samuel lives. Let's ask him if he can help us." As they walked into town, Samuel saw them coming. He came to meet them!

April 5

GOD HAD TOLD SAMUEL that he would soon meet the young man who would be the first king of Israel. As soon as Samuel saw young Saul, he knew this was the man God had been talking about. Before Saul could ask about the lost donkeys, Samuel told him they had already been found. Then the great leader surprised Saul even more. He asked Saul to be his special guest at a big dinner.

The next morning, before Saul left, Samuel told him, "God has chosen you to be the king of his people." Then Samuel poured olive oil over Saul's head to show that God wanted him to be king.

APRIL 6

SAMUEL CALLED God's people together so he could tell them about their new king. But when he looked around for Saul, the young man had disappeared! The people asked God where Saul was. "Hiding among the baggage," God told them. Soon they found Saul and brought him out. Then everyone saw how tall he was. "Here is your king!" cried Samuel, and the crowd cheered. Samuel wrote down a list of rules for the new king to obey. Then Samuel sent the people home.

APRIL 7

KING SAUL WAS a good leader. But he relied on Samuel's help. Samuel would talk to God and then tell the king what God wanted him to do. But eventually King Saul began to think he could get along without Samuel. One day the king was getting his soldiers ready for battle. Samuel told Saul to wait seven days for him before going into battle. At the end of the week, Saul decided not to wait anymore. Soon Samuel arrived and was angry with Saul. "Because you have disobeyed God," said Samuel, "your sons won't rule after you. God will find a new king from another family."

APRIL 8

SAMUEL WAS SAD because King Saul wouldn't listen to God. "Go to Bethlehem and visit Jesse," God told Samuel. "One of his sons will become the next king." So Samuel went to see Jesse, who brought out seven of his sons. Samuel was sure one of them should be king. But God told Samuel the next king wouldn't be the tallest or best-looking one. Samuel asked Jesse if he had any other sons. "My youngest, David, is in the fields, watching the sheep," answered Jesse. As soon as Samuel saw David, he knew that the boy was God's choice. So he poured oil on David's head, just as God said.

APRIL 9

AS TIME WENT ON, many of King Saul's soldiers deserted him. Those who were left had no swords or spears with which to fight the Philistines. But Saul's son Jonathan trusted God. He said, "Nothing can stop God. He can win a battle with just a few people!" One day Jonathan and his servant fought with some Philistine soldiers who were guarding a mountain pass. Most of the Philistine soldiers ran for their lives. But Jonathan won the battle because he was brave and trusted God.

APRIL 10

KING SAUL WAS NOT a happy man. Because he didn't obey God, sometimes he became nervous, sad, and afraid. One of Saul's servants thought that David, who played the harp, could make the king feel better. So Saul sent for David. Soon Saul grew to like the young shepherd boy from Bethlehem. David's music always cheered Saul up when he felt gloomy. The king asked David to come live at the palace so he could play his harp whenever the king asked him to.

APRIL 11

EVERYONE STOPPED

to listen when David played his harp. Just as he had done as a young shepherd boy, David sang songs praising God, called "psalms."

One psalm David wrote says God is our shepherd, and we are his sheep. He gives us everything we need. He leads us on peaceful paths, gives us rest, and makes us strong. He also comforts us when bad things happen.

"God's goodness and love will always be with me, and I will live with God forever," sang David.

APRIL 12

KING SAUL'S ARMY was at war again with the Philistines. Everyone was terrified of a huge Philistine giant named Goliath. He was over nine feet tall and very fierce. Every day Goliath yelled, "If one of you can beat me, we will be your slaves. But if your man loses, you will be our slaves!" David was only a young boy, but he wanted to fight Goliath. He told King Saul, "I know I'm small, but I killed lions and bears when I took care of my father's sheep. God kept me safe then. I know he can keep me safe from Goliath!" Finally the king agreed to let David fight Goliath.

APRIL 13

KING SAUL GAVE David a bronze helmet and a metal coat. But the king's armor was too big and too heavy for David. Instead, David ran to a stream and picked out five smooth stones. Then he went to find his enemy. The giant Goliath laughed when he saw young David. But David said, "This is God's battle!" Then he swung one of the stones in his sling at Goliath. It hit the giant right between the eyes, and he fell to the ground, dead! Saul's army cheered loudly as the rest of the Philistines ran away.

APRIL 14

EVERYONE THOUGHT DAVID was very special after he killed Goliath. The people sang and danced happily whenever David walked by. King Saul was jealous of all the attention David was getting. He was afraid the people would want David to be their king instead of him. But that didn't stop Jonathan, Saul's son, from becoming David's friend. Jonathan was a brave soldier, just like David. He gave David his sword, his bow, and his belt to show that he would always be David's friend, no matter what happened.

APRIL 15

ONE DAY WHEN DAVID played his harp for Saul, the king threw his spear at David. But David jumped to one side and wasn't hurt. Next the king sent David out to fight the Philistines, hoping he would be killed. But David won every fight, and the people liked him even more than before. Next Saul told his own men to kill David. But Jonathan begged his father to spare David's life, and Saul agreed. So David was safe for a while. Then one day, as David played his harp, the king got angry and threw his spear at David again. But David moved quickly, and the spear hit the wall instead!

APRIL 16

ONE NIGHT SAUL SENT some soldiers to watch David's house. He told them to kill David the next morning. But David's wife, Michal, was Saul's daughter. She found out about her father's plan. "You must escape tonight!" she told David. Then she helped him climb out a back window. Early the next morning Saul's men waited for David. But he wasn't there! He was on his way to see Samuel. He told Samuel what King Saul had done. Samuel made sure David had a safe place to stay.

APRIL 17

SOON DAVID had to run away from his hiding place because Saul was on his way to kill him. So he went to see Jonathan. His friend promised to find out if Saul still wanted to hurt David. "Wait here in the fields," Jonathan said. "I'll be back to practice shooting my bow and arrow. If my father still wants to kill you, I'll call out, 'Keep going. The arrow is up ahead.' Then you'll know you must leave." When Jonathan learned his father was still planning to kill David, he warned David as he promised. The two friends cried as they quickly said good-bye.

APRIL 18

DAVID WAS IN deep trouble. He couldn't go back to the king's palace, or anywhere else King Saul might easily find him. So he wandered from place to place. Then one day he came to a huge cave. Here was a safe hiding place! Many of the people, who still thought of David as their hero, heard about his cave. People who were upset, in trouble, or had no money came to David for help and advice. Soon around 400 men were living with David in his cave.

APRIL 19

SAUL KEPT LOOKING for David. David was now the leader of about 600 men. They traveled high up in the hills. One day David and his men were resting in another cave. King Saul himself entered the cave, but he didn't know David was there. David could have surprised the king and fought with him. Instead he just crept up behind Saul and cut off a piece of his coat. Then he followed Saul out of the cave. David said, "I could have killed you, but I didn't." Saul began to cry. "David," he said, "you are a better man than I am. I know you'll be a good king."

APRIL 20

NABAL WAS A FARMER who owned many sheep and goats. He was rich, but he was mean and dishonest too. David's men had helped Nabal's shepherds along the way. Now David heard that the shepherds were nearby, shearing their sheep. So David sent his men to ask Nabal for food and supplies. But Nabal refused. "Is this the thanks I get for taking care of his shepherds?" David asked. He got ready to do battle, but then Nabal's kind wife, Abigail, arrived with all kinds of food. She talked David into not fighting with her husband. Soon after that Nabal died. Then David asked Abigail to marry him.

APRIL 21

AT LAST KING SAUL died fighting his old enemies, the Philistines. Only then was it safe for David to go back home. God told David to go to the south part of the country, called Judah, where the people made him king. But Ishbosheth, another of Saul's sons, became king of the north part of Israel. Fights broke out between King David's army and Ishbosheth's army. After many battles, Ishbosheth was killed. And then the 12 tribes of Israel asked David to rule over the whole land. David was just 30 years old when he became king of all Israel.

121

APRIL 22

AFTER DAVID became king, he decided that Jerusalem would be Israel's new capital city. But some enemies lived in Jerusalem. They laughed at King David and told him, "You'll never get in here. Even people who can't see or walk could keep you out!"

David wasn't going to let those words stop him! He told his troops to go through the tunnels that carried water into Jerusalem. "Once you are inside the city, open the gates for the rest of us," David said. That's how David's army took the city from their enemies. And Jerusalem became known as the "City of David."

APRIL 23

IT HAD BEEN MANY YEARS since David killed Goliath, the Philistine giant. But the Philistines were still enemies of David and God's people. When King David heard the enemy soldiers were coming after him, David wasn't afraid. He asked God what to do.

"Go and fight your old enemies," God said. "I will give you the victory!"

David obeyed God. And he won the battle just as God said he would!

April 24

KING DAVID REMEMBERED to thank God for his goodness. David knew he had become king and won the battle with the Philistines only because that was God's plan. David wanted Jerusalem to be God's holy city. So he gave an order to bring the ark of the covenant into the city. The king and his people danced and played music and sang songs of praise to God. The ark was placed in a special tent. Then David gave special cakes to every person in Israel.

APRIL 25

DAVID NEVER FORGOT

his good friend Jonathan, son of King Saul. They had promised to do whatever they could to take care of each other's families. Now Jonathan was gone. He had been killed in the same battle as his father. It was time for David to keep his promise. He found out that Jonathan had a son named Mephibosheth. He was a grown man with a son of his own, but he was crippled and couldn't walk. King David sent for Mephibosheth. The king said he could live at the palace, just as if he were part of the king's family.

Mephibosheth was so happy! David showed such kindness to Jonathan's son because David and Jonathan had been best friends many years earlier.

APRIL 26

IN THE SPRING King David's army was away at war. But David stayed behind in Jerusalem. One day, from his roof garden, he saw a beautiful woman taking a bath. "What is her name?" he asked his servant. "Bathsheba," answered the servant. "She is the wife of one of your best soldiers." David called for Bathsheba to come to the palace. He slept with her as if she were his wife, even though he knew it was wrong. Soon Bathsheba sent David a message that she was going to have a baby. David quickly sent her husband to the front of a big battle, where he was killed. Then David married Bathsheba.

APRIL 27

GOD WASN'T HAPPY with David for killing a man and taking his wife. So God sent the prophet Nathan to the palace with this story for the king. "Two men lived in a town. One man was rich, and the other was poor. The rich man had everything he needed, but he took and killed the only thing the poor man really loved—his lamb." Then Nathan told David, "You are like that rich man. You stole Bathsheba from her husband, but she was all he had." Now David felt very sorry for what he had done. He prayed a long prayer, asking God to forgive him.

127

APRIL 28

ABSALOM, ONE of David's sons, wanted to be the next king of Israel more than anything. But he didn't want to wait until his father died. Absalom got to know the people of Israel. He helped them with their problems. He wanted the people to like him more than David so they would choose him to be their king. By the time David learned what was going on, even his closest friends were on Absalom's side. David was very upset. So he made plans to leave Jerusalem before Absalom and his followers took over the city. He told the priests to take the ark of the covenant out of the city too, and set it down beside the road.

April 29

DAVID NEVER stopped trusting God. While he was away from Jerusalem, he sent the ark back to the city. "If God still wants me to be king, he will bring me back safely too," he said. Battles broke out between Absalom's men and David's soldiers. David still loved his son and didn't want him to get hurt. When Absalom was killed by some of David's soldiers, David was heartbroken. Then, since there was no reason to fight anymore, David thanked his troops for their help. The people asked him to come back to Jerusalem as their king. This made David happy again. He said, "I am once again the king!"

APRIL 30

KING DAVID WAS NOW an old man, and his son Adonijah wanted to take over. So Adonijah appointed  himself as the new king. But he didn't tell his father because he knew David had never said anything about him being the next king. When the prophet Nathan heard what was going on, he talked to Bathsheba, the mother of King David's son Solomon. She reminded David that he had promised to make Solomon the next king. David immediately gave the order for Solomon to be the new king. The people shouted and blew trumpets when they heard this news. Then Adonijah was afraid! But Solomon told him to stop trying to be king and come home.

MAY 1

KING DAVID TOLD Solomon all he knew about how to be a good king. But before long, David died, leaving Solomon to be the new king of Israel. One night Solomon had a dream. In this dream God asked him, "What would you like me to give you?" Right away Solomon said, "What I need most is to be wise. I can't rule the people without your help." God was pleased with Solomon's answer. So he promised to give Solomon much more than he asked for. Besides making him wise, God promised that Solomon would be rich and have a long life if he obeyed God's laws.

131

MAY 2

PEOPLE CAME FROM all over to ask King Solomon's advice. One day two women brought a baby boy to him. Each woman claimed the child belonged to her. They wanted Solomon to decide which one of them was the real mother. So Solomon said, "Cut this baby in two and give half to each of these women." One of the women cried, "No! Don't hurt the baby! I would rather give him up than see him hurt." But the other woman said, "Go ahead, divide him between us!" Solomon

knew right away that the woman who wanted to keep the baby safe was the real mother. The baby was hers! This story spread quickly, and soon everyone was in awe of the great wisdom God had given Solomon.

MAY 3

AFTER SOLOMON

became king, there was peace in Israel. Now it was time to build a special house for God called a temple. Here the people could all worship God together. King Solomon made plans to build the most beautiful temple ever. He asked his father's good friend, King Hiram of Tyre, for help. Hiram gladly gave Solomon all the wood he needed from his many cedar and cypress trees. Solomon hired thousands of workers to saw the wood and cut stones. After the huge temple was built, the workers made it even more beautiful by covering it with jewels and shiny gold. After seven long years of hard work, the wonderful temple was finally finished!

MAY 4

WHEREVER PEOPLE WENT, they told stories about Solomon's wisdom and wealth. Soon kings and queens from far away heard these stories. The queen of Sheba wanted to find out if these stories about a rich, wise king were really true. So she rode a camel for many miles to visit Solomon. Other camels came with her, carrying expensive gifts. When she arrived at King Solomon's palace, she saw with her own eyes how rich he was! She asked him many hard questions, and he gave wise answers. At the end of her visit, the queen knew everything she'd heard about Solomon was true!

MAY 5

WHEN SOLOMON LIVED, men had the right to marry more than one woman. But instead of choosing women who loved God, King Solomon began to marry women who worshiped other gods. Solomon knew that God said it was wrong to worship idols. That's what his father, David, had taught him. And David had been a good, wise king. But little by little, Solomon stopped listening to God. He began to worship his wives' gods. That made God sad and angry. Solomon no longer chose to obey God, and that got him in trouble!

MAY 6

BECAUSE KING Solomon no longer obeyed God, God told him that none of his sons would be king over the whole country of Israel. Instead, one of Solomon's servants would become the king of part of the country. And that's exactly what happened. When Solomon died, his son Rehoboam thought he'd be king of all Israel. But because he wasn't a kind leader, the people said, "We want Jeroboam the servant to rule us instead!" Israel was split into two kingdoms. Rehoboam became king of Judah, which was only one tiny part of the kingdom. And Jeroboam became king of the biggest part of Israel. So God's words came true. Because Solomon had stopped obeying God, God took most of the big, rich kingdom away from his family.

MAY 7

GOD'S PROPHETS, his special messengers, warned Jeroboam to obey God. But Jeroboam didn't listen. One day Jeroboam's son got very sick. Jeroboam was worried. So he sent his wife, the queen, to visit an old prophet who could tell people what was going to happen next. The queen pretended to be a poor woman. The prophet was almost blind, but God told him who the visitor was. "Come in," the old man said. "But why are you pretending to be someone else?" Then he told her God would punish Jeroboam's family because of his disobedience.

MAY 8

THE MOST EVIL RULER Israel had ever had was King Ahab. Instead of obeying God, he did many wrong things. Ahab's wife, Queen Jezebel, even talked him into building a temple to worship another god named Baal. God was very unhappy. He was angry with Ahab because Ahab had made the people forget about the only true God. Now they worshiped other gods, called idols. So he sent the wise prophet Elijah to warn King Ahab about what God was going to do.

MAY 9

THE PROPHET ELIJAH wanted to obey the one true God. So when Elijah went to see the evil King Ahab, he was honest with him. He told the king he needed to learn to obey God. Until this happened, Elijah said, "There will be no more rain until I say so." Ahab was very angry with Elijah. So God told Elijah to go hide at a place called Kerith Brook. Over the next few years, there was almost nothing to eat or drink in the country of Israel. But God sent big black ravens to bring food to Elijah. And he always had plenty of water to drink at the brook.

MAY 10

IT DIDN'T RAIN in Israel for a long time. Even the brook where the prophet Elijah had been hiding dried up. So God told Elijah to go to the town of Zarephath. "A widow there will feed you," God said. Elijah met the woman and asked her for some food. She said sadly, "I have just enough flour and oil to make one small loaf for my son and me before we starve!" Elijah told her to bake a loaf for him first, and then another for herself.

"God has promised you'll never run out of flour and oil," he said. They all ate from her supply for many days. And there was always enough!

MAY 11

ELIJAH STAYED AT THE woman's home in Zarephath. One day her son became very sick. He grew worse and worse, and finally he died. Elijah said, "Give your son to me." He carried the boy upstairs and laid him on his bed. Then he prayed three times for the boy to live again. God heard Elijah and brought the boy back to life! The boy's mother was so happy. She told Elijah, "Now I know that you have been sent by God and that God speaks through you. Everything he tells you to say is true."

141

MAY 12

THREE YEARS without rain didn't make King Ahab and Queen Jezebel change their evil ways. One day Elijah told King Ahab, "Let's see whose god is real!" So the king and his prophets met Elijah on a mountaintop. Elijah told the king's prophets to pray for fire to burn up their gift to their god. So the prophets prayed and prayed. But nothing happened because their god wasn't real and couldn't hear them. Then Elijah poured water over his gift and asked God to set it on fire. Hot flames shot down right away from heaven! When the people saw the fire, they knew what Elijah said was true—that there was only one real God.

MAY 13

EVIL QUEEN JEZEBEL wanted to kill Elijah. So he ran away and hid in a cave. He felt sad and lonely. Was he the only one left on earth who loved God? And where was God when he was in trouble?

Suddenly the wind began to howl. But God wasn't in the wind. Soon the ground shook. But God wasn't in the earthquake. Next there was a fire. But God wasn't in the fire. Then, when all grew quiet, Elijah heard a gentle whisper. "Keep working for me," God said. "You aren't alone. I'll show you!"

MAY 14

A PROPHET'S LIFE was often hard and lonely. But God knew just the right person to help Elijah. His name sounded a lot like Elijah's name! "Go and look for a young man named Elisha," God told Elijah. "Pour oil over his head to show that he is the one who will do your work after you have gone." Elijah obeyed God and found Elisha plowing his father's field. Elisha knew right away that God wanted him to follow Elijah. And Elisha knew there would be no turning back. "First let me kiss my parents good-bye," he said. "Then I will go with you!"

He ate one last meal with his friends and then went with Elijah to be his helper.

MAY 15

CLOSE TO AHAB'S PALACE was a garden where a man called Naboth grew grapes. King Ahab wanted to own this land. He said he would pay for it, but Naboth wouldn't sell it. "It belongs to my family," he told the king. Ahab was so angry that he went to bed without eating! When Jezebel saw how upset he was, she said she would get the land for him. So Jezebel wrote to

the city leaders, ordering them to kill Naboth. Then she signed the letters with the king's name. Naboth was killed. Soon after that God sent Elijah to see King Ahab. "God will bring great trouble to you and your family for what you have done," said Elijah.

MAY 16

FOR THREE YEARS there was no war. Then the evil King Ahab wanted to win back the city of Ramoth-gilead, which belonged to Israel. Ahab asked King Jehoshaphat of Judah to help. Jehoshaphat, who obeyed God, said, "First let's find out if God thinks we should go to war or not." So King Ahab called four hundred of his prophets. They all said what they knew King Ahab wanted to hear. "Go ahead! God will let you win." Only the prophet Micaiah said what God told him to say.

"If you go to war, God will not help you win. And you won't live through the battle. The other prophets are lying to you."

146

MAY 17

KING AHAB NEVER LISTENED to God. Ignoring the prophet Micaiah's warning, Ahab sent his army off to fight. He put on different clothes so no one would recognize him. Then he followed his soldiers in a chariot. During the battle, an enemy soldier shot an arrow at Ahab's soldiers. The arrow hit and killed Ahab instead. But the good king, Jehoshaphat of Judah, lived through the war because he did everything he could to please God. After King Ahab's death, Jehoshaphat ruled his country for many more years. He also made peace with the next king of Israel.

147

MAY 18

ELIJAH WAS OUT walking with his young helper, Elisha. Both men knew this would be Elijah's last day on earth. Three times the old prophet said he wanted to walk on by himself. He tried to talk Elisha into staying behind. But each time Elisha said, "As long as you live, I'll never leave you!"

"What can I do for you before I am taken away?" Elijah finally asked Elisha.

Elisha said, "Pass on to me twice as much power as you have from God."

Elijah told him, "If you see me when I am taken from you up to heaven, then God will give you what you've asked."

MAY 19

AS THE PROPHETS

Elijah and Elisha were walking together, Elisha suddenly saw a chariot of fire in the sky! As it drove toward Elijah the wind began to howl. The chariot twisted and turned and carried Elijah up to heaven. Elisha called to him, but the old man was gone. Only his coat was left on the ground. Elisha picked up the coat, feeling very sad. He walked slowly back to the Jordan River. He stopped by the river, rolled up Elijah's coat, and hit the water with it. The river parted in two so he could walk across! Then Elisha knew he had God's power and could carry on Elijah's work.

MAY 20

A GROUP OF prophets watched as Elisha parted the waters of the Jordan River. "Now God's power is with Elisha!" they said. News spread that Elisha had taken over the Elijah's work. Some men from Jericho came to see Elisha. They said, "Something is wrong with the water in our town. It makes us sick, and no crops will grow in our fields." Elisha asked them for a bowl of salt. Then he threw the salt into the spring where the town's water came from. "Now the water will be clean," Elisha said. And sure enough, Jericho's water was safe and good from then on!

MAY 21

ONE DAY A WIDOW came to see Elisha. "Before my husband died, he borrowed some money from a man," she said. "Now the man wants me to pay him back. He will make my two sons his slaves if I don't. Please help me, because I have no money! All I have is one small jar of oil." Elisha told her to borrow as many empty jars as she could from her neighbors. "Then pour your oil into them," Elisha said. The oil from the woman's one small jar didn't run out until all the jars were full! "Sell the oil," Elisha said, "and pay the man what you owe. You'll never be poor again."

151

MAY 22

ELISHA traveled from place to place, teaching God's people. When he visited the town of Shunem, a rich woman invited him to her home for a meal. She and her husband decided to build a comfortable guest room in their home so Elisha would have a place to stay whenever he was in town. Elisha wanted to do something to help the woman for being so kind. He knew she didn't have any children, and he knew all her money couldn't buy a child. So Elisha said to the woman, "This time next year you'll be holding a baby son in your arms." The woman was afraid to believe him. But one year later, Elisha's words came true!

MAY 23

THE RICH WOMAN and her husband loved their son. One day he went out to the field to see his father. Suddenly he began to cry because his head hurt so much. His father told one of his helpers to carry the boy home. The mother held him, but she couldn't help him. He died, and the woman quietly carried the boy upstairs. Then she got on a donkey and rode as fast as she could to find Elisha. Elisha came back to her house. He prayed that God would bring the child back to life. Then he touched the boy. The little boy sneezed seven times and then opened his eyes! How happy everyone was!

153

MAY 24

GOD TOLD ELISHA there would be a famine in Israel. No crops would grow for seven years. So Elisha told his kind friends in Shunem, "Until the famine is over, go and find somewhere else to live." So the family traveled to the land of the Philistines, where they lived for seven years. When the crops began growing again, the family went back home.

But some strangers now lived in their house. The mother went to the king for help. The king was amazed because he had just heard how Elisha had brought the woman's son back to life! So the king helped her get her house back as well as the value of the crops sold while she was away. God took good care of the kind woman and her family!

MAY 25

NAAMAN, THE LEADER of the Aramean army, had painful sores all over his skin. He didn't know what to do. But a servant girl from Israel told Naaman's wife, "Elisha, a prophet of God from my country, could make your husband well." So Naaman traveled to Israel to find the prophet. Elisha told him to wash seven times in the Jordan River. At first Naaman was angry. He didn't want to wash in the dirty river. But his men told him to obey Elisha. After going into the water seven times, the sores on Naaman's skin disappeared! He ran to thank Elisha, saying, "Now I know at last that Israel's God is the only real God in the world!"

MAY 26

ISRAEL FOUGHT WITH the country of Aram. The king of Aram was upset. "A spy is giving our secrets away," he said. His officers thought it was Elisha. They thought he was helping the king of Israel. So the king of Aram sent his troops to capture Elisha. The enemy soldiers surrounded the city where Elisha was staying. As they were about to grab him, Elisha asked God to make the soldiers blind. And God did! Then Elisha led the enemy soldiers to his king. He prayed they could see again. And they did! He told the king to feed them and then send them home. After this, the Aramean army stayed away from Israel.

MAY 27

JOASH BECAME KING OF JUDAH when
he was only seven years old. His grandmother had ruled
the land before him, but she was a cruel and evil queen.
The people were happy to have a good king at last, even
though he was only a child. Joash grew up loving God,
and he wanted his people to love God
too. While Joash's grandmother
was queen, the temple had
been damaged. When King
Joash grew older, he made sure
it was repaired. He told the
people to bring money to
the temple to pay the
workers who helped
make the building
beautiful again. The
workers made the
temple a special place for
worship once more.

MAY 28

GOD WASN'T HAPPY with the people who lived in the city of Nineveh. They disobeyed him and did many bad things. Jonah was one of God's special prophets. God told Jonah to go to Nineveh and warn the people to change their ways. But Jonah didn't want to do as God asked. Instead he ran away and tried to hide from God. He went to the town of Joppa and got on a boat going to Tarshish. This was about as far away from Nineveh as Jonah could hope to get. Then, tired out from his travels, Jonah fell asleep in the bottom of the boat.

MAY 29

THE BIG BOAT sailed out to sea. Then God sent a terrible storm. Huge waves rocked the boat, and the sailors were afraid they were going to die. They woke up Jonah, who was sleeping. "It's my fault," Jonah said. "I was trying to run away from God. Throw me over the side of the boat." When the men did, the storm stopped right away!

MAY 30

GOD DIDN'T LET Jonah drown in the sea. Instead he sent a big fish to swallow Jonah whole! Jonah spent three days and three nights inside the fish. He had plenty of time to think about what he'd done, and now he was sorry he hadn't obeyed God. Jonah thanked God for keeping him safe. After the third day, the fish swam close to land, and God told it to spit Jonah out on the shore. Then God told Jonah again to go to the city of Nineveh.

MAY 31

JONAH TOLD THE PEOPLE of Nineveh to tell God they were sorry for their sins. And they did! Jonah was angry because God forgave them immediately without punishing them first. As Jonah sat and sulked in the shade of a vine, God decided to teach him another lesson. He sent a worm to eat the vine until it died. Now Jonah had no more shade. "I'm so hot and angry that I want to die!" cried Jonah.

"You're sorry this plant died," said God. "I feel even more sorry for thousands of people in Ninevah who would have died if they hadn't told me they were sorry!"

JUNE 1

JOASH, KING OF THE southern kingdom of Judah, was a wise ruler for many years. He taught his people to obey God. But little by little he began to listen to those who didn't love God. Soon he wasn't a good king anymore. After Joash, most of the kings of Judah weren't good kings either. King Ahaz even stole silver and gold from God's temple. Bad kings also ruled in the northern kingdom of Israel. They did many evil things, and they all worshiped idols instead of God. Before long, no one in Israel, north or south, remembered God or tried to obey him. This was a sad time for God's people.

162

JUNE 2

GOD WAS VERY ANGRY at the people of Israel and Judah. They had forgotten everything God had done for them. Had God saved them all from slavery in Egypt and brought them into the Promised Land for nothing? Time after time, God told his people to stop worshiping gods that weren't real and turn back to him. But no one listened. They built places to worship idols and did many bad things. So God let the kingdom of Israel in the north be captured by their enemies. The people had to go and live far away in another land called Assyria. And their children still live there today!

JUNE 3

KING HEZEKIAH ruled over the land of Judah in the south. Unlike his father, Ahaz, Hezekiah loved God. King Ahaz had closed the doors of the temple, so no one worshiped God there anymore. As soon as Hezekiah became king, he had the temple cleaned. It took 16 days to prepare the temple for worship. Then there was a special service. People gave many gifts to God, and sang and played trumpets!

JUNE 4

NOW THAT THE TEMPLE could be used again, King Hezekiah wanted as many people as possible to worship God there. Passover was a very special time—a time for God's people to remember how he saved them from being slaves in Egypt. Hezekiah asked everyone in all of Israel and Judah to come to Jerusalem for Passover. Huge crowds traveled to the city. The people worshiped God together for two whole weeks! Then the people helped King Hezekiah destroy many idols and places for worshiping idols. They wanted to worship only the true God.

JUNE 5

KING HEZEKIAH ALWAYS tried to obey God and do what was right. Because of this, he was successful, even when he faced big problems. When the king of Assyria ordered his army to invade Judah and attack Jerusalem, Hezekiah talked with the leaders of his army. They decided to block off the springs of water in the ground outside the city. This made the brook that flowed through the fields dry up. "Why should the Assyrians come here and find plenty of water?" they said. Hezekiah's army also fixed up the broken wall around the city. They even built a second wall outside the first one!

JUNE 6

HEZEKIAH called the people of Jerusalem together. "Be brave!" he said. "The king of Assyria has a huge army, but we are stronger than he is because God is on our side." Soon after that, the enemy leaders arrived. They tried to make Hezekiah and his people afraid. "What makes you think your God will save you?" the Assyrian king said. "We always win every fight with our enemies."

Hezekiah prayed to God for help. And God sent an angel to fight the enemy army. The king of Assyria lost the fight and went home. People from all over Judah brought gifts to Jerusalem to thank God for keeping his people safe.

June 7

For more than 70 years after Hezekiah, God's people worshiped idols again. Then Hezekiah's great-grandson, Josiah, became king. He was just eight years old! And he was a good king, just like Hezekiah had been. Josiah destroyed all the idols and

began fixing up God's temple, which the people had neglected. One day the priest Hilkiah found the Book of the Law with the commandments God had given to Moses. King Josiah listened sadly as the laws were read out loud. He said, "We have disobeyed God. We haven't been doing what the Book says we must do!"

JUNE 8

HILKIAH THE PRIEST and some of the king's officers went to see Huldah, a prophet. They wanted to hear what she had to say about the Book of the Law. She told the men to give King Josiah this message. "God says he's angry at the people for not obeying him," she began. "He will destroy the city of Jerusalem because the people have worshiped false gods and have forgotten his laws. But because King Josiah obeys God and is sorry for what the people have done, this won't happen until his life is over."

JUNE 9

THE KING'S OFFICERS listened to Huldah the prophet and told King Josiah what she had said. Right away the king called all the people to the temple in Jerusalem. Everyone was asked to come, even the most important leaders and the poorest people. King Josiah read the whole Book of the Law to the crowd. Then the king promised to obey all of God's laws with all his heart. And he told the people, "Each one of you must also promise to do what God's laws say." After that, for as long as Josiah ruled Judah, the people obeyed God.

JUNE 10

JEREMIAH, HILKIAH'S SON, was learning to be a priest. One day Jeremiah heard God say, "You must go where I send you. Be my special messenger, and I'll give you words to pass along to the people."

"Don't send me!" said Jeremiah. "I'm too young!"

"Don't be afraid," said God. "I'll be with you." He touched Jeremiah's mouth. "Now I've put the words in your mouth that I want you to say."

God knew his people didn't love him. So he told Jeremiah to warn them that the south kingdom of Israel, called Judah, would soon be destroyed.

JUNE 11

MANY TIMES THE prophet Jeremiah warned the people of Judah to stop doing bad things. He said if they were sorry for what they did, God would forgive them and not let the enemy soldiers take over Jerusalem. But no one listened. So God told Jeremiah to write down all the messages he had ever given the people. "If you read these messages to the people, maybe they will be sorry," God said. The messages were read to the people at the temple and to King Zedekiah in his palace. But the king wasn't sorry. He was angry. He cut up Jeremiah's writings and threw them into a fire. Then God told Jeremiah to write the messages again. Jeremiah wrote everything out again, and added even more this time!

JUNE 12

YEARS LATER, GOD SPOKE again to the prophet Jeremiah. The powerful king of Babylon was coming with his army to fight against the city of Jerusalem. God said to Jeremiah, "Go and tell King Zedekiah that I will soon give this city to the enemy. The city will be burned to the ground and the king will be taken prisoner. But I promise that Zedekiah won't be killed in war. He will die quietly and be buried with honor." Even though Jeremiah knew the king wouldn't like the message, Jeremiah obeyed God. He gave the message to the king.

JUNE 13

KING ZEDEKIAH and the people of Judah didn't want to hear Jeremiah's gloomy messages about the city of Jerusalem. They didn't believe the messages were from God. One day some of the king's men threw Jeremiah down a deep, dark well to keep him quiet. There was no water in the well, only thick mud. But an officer from the palace heard what happened to Jeremiah. He told the king, "Set Jeremiah free, or he will die."

So the king sent 30 men to help lift Jeremiah out of the dirty well. They took him to the palace prison, where he stayed.

JUNE 14

EVERYTHING Jeremiah said would happen to Judah finally did. The king of Babylon and his army crashed through the city walls to take over Jerusalem. King Zedekiah tried to escape at night through the palace garden, but enemy soldiers found him. They blinded him and put chains around him. Then they took him far away to Babylon. But the king of Babylon was kind to Jeremiah, God's prophet. "Don't hurt him," he told his servants. "Give him whatever he wants." Soon Jeremiah was set free to be with the people who were left in Judah.

JUNE 15

JERUSALEM WAS IN big trouble. So God told Ezekiel to show the people what was going to happen. Ezekiel drew a picture of the city of Jerusalem on a large clay brick. He made ramps from clay and placed them around the brick. Then he put an iron plate between himself and the brick, like a wall. This showed how the people would be trapped in their own city. Ezekiel also began baking and eating a tiny loaf of bread each day and drinking only two tiny cups of water. Soon the people would have only that to eat and drink too. All this would happen because they wouldn't obey God!

June 16

GOD OFTEN TALKED to his special messengers, the prophets, through dreams. The prophet Ezekiel had a daydream. He saw a dark storm cloud with fire in the middle. As Ezekiel watched, a huge machine came out of the cloud. It had wheels so it could move

fast on land and wings so it could fly through the air. Each of the four sides of the machine was a different creature, with a different face. And in the middle sat a man on a throne, with a rainbow all around him. Ezekiel bowed low to the ground. He knew God was right there with him!

JUNE 17

GOD'S PEOPLE WERE very unhappy. They hadn't obeyed God, and now they had to live near the city of Babylon, far away from their own country. They didn't feel like playing their harps or singing happy songs the way they used to. Instead, they sang this sad song:

We sat down by the rivers of Babylon and cried as we thought of Jerusalem.

How can we sing the songs of the Lord while in a foreign land?

178

JUNE 18

EZEKIEL TOLD THE PEOPLE that God had talked to him in a dream. "I was in a valley filled with hundreds of bones," Ezekiel said. "God told me he was going to put skin on these dry bones and bring the people back to life. Suddenly I saw the bones join together to form skeletons. Skin began to cover the skeletons, and soon the valley was filled with human bodies. God said I should tell the winds to breathe life into these bodies. So I did, and the dead people began to breathe again. Then God told me that someday he will bring his people back home again. It will be like they have come back to life."

JUNE 19

JOB WAS A rich farmer. He had lots of sheep, camels, oxen, and donkeys. And he had a large, happy family. Job prayed all the time for his children. Job was honest and good. He obeyed God in everything he did. And that made God happy!

One day Satan, the enemy of God, told God, "Job only obeys you because of the good things you do for him." So God told Satan he could take everything away from Job.

Soon terrible things started happening to Job. All his farm animals were killed or stolen. And a desert wind storm took the lives of his children. Job was very sad, but he still loved God and obeyed him.

June 20

JOB GOT TERRIBLE sores all over his body, but Job still said, "We let God send good things. We must also let him send trouble." Three of Job's friends came to see him. "Stop doing bad things. Tell God you are sorry for your sins," they said. Job knew he had done nothing wrong. But he did wonder why God had let so many bad things happen to him. Finally, during a storm, God spoke to Job. He helped Job understand that he could trust God to do what was right. Then God sent good things to Job again—even more animals and a bigger family than before!

JUNE 21

NEBUCHADNEZZAR was the king of Babylon who defeated Jerusalem when Jeremiah lived there. He told his officers to bring back some strong, nice-looking young men who could learn new things and be trained to become good leaders. Daniel and his three friends were four of the young men chosen. These four friends were far from home, but they still wanted to obey God. They knew that God didn't want them to eat the king's rich food. So they asked if they could have just vegetables and water. The man in charge let them have the food they asked for. And they became stronger than all the other young men!

JUNE 22

ONE DAY the king of Babylon told his helpers, "I had a strange dream. Tell me what I dreamed and what it means, or you will die." So Daniel asked God to tell him about the king's dream and then went to see the king.

"God told me you dreamed about a statue with a gold head and feet of clay," Daniel said. "A great stone smashed the statue. This is what it means. You are like the statue's head, ruling over the whole world. The clay feet are like a weak kingdom following yours. But someday God will set up a kingdom that will last forever. That kingdom is like the stone in your dream. It will crush all other kingdoms."

"If you know this," the king said, "your God must be the one and only God."

JUNE 23

THE KING of Babylon couldn't forget his dream. He thought it would be great to have a real statue of himself, made of gold from head to toe. So the king ordered the people to make the statue. When the statue was finished, it was quite a sight. Shining brightly in the sunlight, the huge figure stood as tall as 15 men standing on top of each other.

"All people must worship my statue," said the king. "They must do this when they hear the music of horns and flutes and harps. Anyone who won't worship my statue will be thrown into a hot furnace!"

JUNE 24

DANIEL'S THREE FRIENDS, Shadrach, Meshach, and Abednego, wouldn't bow down to the king of Babylon's gold statue. They said bravely, "We worship only God."

"Throw them into the fire," shouted the king. So they were thrown into a hot furnace. But the king saw not three, but four people in the fire. And one looked like an angel! The king quickly ordered the three friends to come out of the furnace. They walked out, not hurt at all. And the fourth figure was gone! Now the king worshiped God. He wouldn't let anyone say anything bad about the three men or their God.

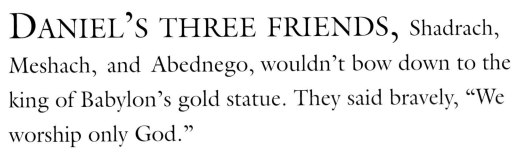

JUNE 25

KING NEBUCHADNEZZAR had another strange dream. In his dream, the king saw a very tall tree. "Cut down this tree," ordered an angel. The tree stump turned into a man. "This man must live like a wild animal," said the angel. "He has to learn that God rules the world." Daniel was able to explain this dream to King Nebuchadnezzar. "You are like the tree," he said. "If you don't obey God, you will lose your power." But the king wouldn't obey God. So he had to leave the palace and live out in the country like an animal for many years, just like in his dream. When at last he returned to his palace, he always honored God and obeyed him.

JUNE 26

SEVERAL YEARS later, King Belshazzar gave a big dinner party. Belshazzar asked for the gold cups that had been taken from God's temple in Jerusalem. Everyone drank from these cups, which were to be used only when worshiping God. Suddenly the king saw a hand—without an arm!—writing on the wall. The king became very afraid! Only Daniel knew what the words meant.

"Because you chose not to obey God, your days as king will soon end," said Daniel.

That very night Belshazzar was killed, and King Darius took his place.

JUNE 27

THE NEW KING, Darius, chose Daniel to be his most important helper. This made some of the other men who worked for the king angry. They didn't want Daniel to be more important than they were. So they made plans to get rid of him. They went to the king and said, "We think you should make a law that says people can pray only to you for a whole month. If they pray to God, they will be thrown to the lions." The king liked this idea, so he passed the new law. Then no one, not even the king himself, could change it. But that didn't stop Daniel. He had always prayed to God, and so he kept praying three times every day.

JUNE 28

DANIEL'S ENEMIES told the king that Daniel was breaking the new law. King Darius didn't want to hurt Daniel, but even the king had to obey his own law. So he had Daniel thrown into the lions' den. But the king said to Daniel, "May God keep you safe!" The next morning, the king ran to the lions' den. He asked Daniel, "Was your God able to save you?" Daniel answered, "Yes, God sent an angel to close the lions' mouths!" The king had Daniel removed from the lions' den. There wasn't even a scratch on him! Then the king made a new law, telling all the people to honor Daniel's God.

JUNE 29

GOD'S PEOPLE were called Jews. Some of the Jews were living in a faraway city in the Persian Empire. The powerful ruler of this large empire was King Xerxes. He always expected his orders to be obeyed. So one time when his beautiful wife, Queen Vashti, wouldn't obey him, she was sent away forever. Soon Xerxes began looking for a new queen. A group of young women gathered in the palace so the king could choose which one he wanted. One of them was Esther, a young Jewish woman who was beautiful and also gentle and kind. As soon as the king saw Esther, he loved her. He chose her to be his queen.

JUNE 30

HAMAN, AN IMPORTANT leader in King Xerxes' court, hated the Jews. He especially didn't like it when a Jewish man named Mordecai wouldn't bow down to him. So he came up with an evil plan to murder all of the Jews. He said to the king, "Your Majesty, the Jews make trouble and don't obey your laws. If you let me set a date to kill them, I promise to give the royal treasury a lot of money."

"Keep the money," the king said. "Just go ahead and do what you like with these people." But the king had no idea that his own wife, Queen Esther, was a Jew too!

JULY 1

ESTHER'S COUSIN MORDECAI worked at the king's palace. When he heard about Haman's evil plan to kill the Jews, he was very sad. He sent a message to Queen Esther. "You must ask the king to save the Jewish people!" Esther knew she'd be in danger if she went to see the king without being asked. She could even be killed! "If you don't go to him, you'll die anyway," Mordecai said. "Maybe you became queen to save your people!" So Esther bravely went to see the king. And he was happy to see her!

JULY 2

KING XERXES ASKED Queen Esther how he could help her. "I want you and Haman to come to a banquet I've prepared for you," said Esther. So they went to Esther's party. Esther asked the men to eat with her again the next night. During the second banquet, she told the king, "There's a man who plans to kill all my people."

"Who would do such a thing?" asked the king. Esther pointed to Haman. Haman grew pale with fright, and the king became very angry. "Haman must die!" the king shouted.

Before long all the Jews were safe. Because Esther was brave, she saved her people.

JULY 3

GOD'S PEOPLE LIVED in Babylon for a long time. When Cyrus became king, everything changed. God told Cyrus to send a letter to everyone.

"God has told me to build him a temple in Jerusalem," the letter read. "All of God's people may return to Jerusalem to rebuild this temple. And their neighbors should help them by giving them silver, gold, and supplies for their journey."

King Cyrus also made sure that the treasures that had been stolen from God's temple were sent back to Jerusalem.

JULY 4

GOD'S PEOPLE were very happy to return to Jerusalem. Huge crowds gathered in the city to watch the priests build an altar and offer gifts to God.

After many days of celebration, the people began the hard work of building the temple. When the first stones were put in place, the people danced and sang for joy. Some of the older priests cried because they remembered the first temple. The joyful songs and the sad cries were so loud they could be heard far away.

JULY 5

AFTER MANY YEARS, the temple was rebuilt. But God's people needed a new leader to teach them about God and his laws. So God chose Ezra, who lived in Babylon, to be their leader and teacher. Ezra knew God's laws and wanted to obey them.

When Ezra left Babylon to go to Jerusalem, the king of Persia gave him everything he asked for. He even sent a letter with Ezra telling everyone to be generous and help him in his work at the temple.

JULY 6

THERE WAS STILL a lot of work to be done in Jerusalem. Even though the temple had been rebuilt, the walls of the city were still broken. So Jerusalem wasn't safe from its enemies. Nehemiah was an Israelite who had stayed in Babylon. He was a servant of the king of Persia. He wanted to help his people in Jerusalem. So Nehemiah prayed, "O God, I'm sorry for all the times your people haven't obeyed you. Please remember your promise to bring us back together again, in one place, if we obey you. And please let the king allow me to go help build Jerusalem!"

197

July 7

The king of Persia was surprised. Nehemiah had never looked sad before. "What's wrong?" asked the king. "Are you sick? Or has something upset you?"

Nehemiah didn't want to make the king angry. He had been praying that God would help him know what to say and when to say it. So Nehemiah said, "I'm sad because Jerusalem, the city of my people, is in trouble. And I'd like to go help my people. Would you allow me to go?"

The king said yes, and Nehemiah knew God had answered his prayer! Nehemiah quickly made plans to leave for Jerusalem.

JULY 8

THE KING OF PERSIA helped Nehemiah get ready to go to Jerusalem. The king wrote letters to the rulers of the countries Nehemiah would travel through, asking them to let him pass safely. He sent guards on horses to travel with him. The king even agreed to use wood from his own forest for Jerusalem's gates. When Nehemiah finally arrived in Jerusalem, he didn't tell anyone about his plans for the city right away. He didn't want to make the city's leaders angry. He just wanted to see what needed to be done. So in the middle of the night he went out to look over the city and plan what he should do next.

JULY 9

NEHEMIAH CALLED Jerusalem's leaders together tell them how much work the city needed. "Our city was once so strong. It's sad that now it's just a pile of stones," he said. "Let's rebuild the city walls so we can keep our enemies out!" God's people were happy to help. They all began working hard. But not everyone in Jerusalem wanted God's people to be safe. At first these people just made fun of God's people. But that didn't stop the building. Next these enemies said they would fight the Israelites. So Nehemiah told half of the Israelites to carry swords and spears while the other half worked. But because they prayed, God kept them safe.

JULY 10

LIFE HAD NOT BEEN EASY for God's people since they returned to Jerusalem. Some families had lost everything. They told Nehemiah, "We don't have enough money to buy food. Some of us even had to sell our children as slaves, because we are so poor." Nehemiah was angry. He knew the rich and powerful leaders in Jerusalem had raised taxes and made people pay to borrow money. So Nehemiah ordered them to give back everything they had taken from the people. And he told them they could never charge the people to borrow money again. From then on, Nehemiah made sure the leaders treated the people fairly.

JULY 11

GOD'S PEOPLE WORKED very hard to fix the walls around Jerusalem. They wanted the city to be safe from enemies. Nehemiah divided the people into teams. Each team worked on one section of the wall. Sometimes an entire family worked on one part of the wall. Teams of priests worked on other parts of the wall. People from all around the city came to help. Everyone worked from early morning until late at night. It was hard work, but the people were happy to be doing what God wanted.

July 12

The city of Jerusalem was safe once again. God's people had worked hard and finished the city walls in less than two months. Now their enemies couldn't get into the city. It was time to have a big party! People came to Jerusalem from many different towns. They thanked God and told him that Jerusalem once again

belonged to him. They asked him to keep his people safe. The people were so happy that they danced to the music of harps and cymbals. And they marched around the tops of the new city walls, singing praises to God!

July 13

GOD'S PEOPLE HAD been waiting a long time. They knew God was going to send a special king, a "Messiah," to save his people. But they didn't know how or when the Messiah would come. Then God told the prophet Isaiah about a very special baby who would be born in a human body, but would be God. He would grow up to be called the "Prince of Peace." He would be a good leader and treat all God's people fairly. At last Isaiah's words came true. God came to earth as a baby.

JULY 14

GOD SENT THE ANGEL Gabriel to Nazareth to visit a young woman named Mary. The angel told her, "Don't be frightened, for God has decided to bless you. You will have a baby, and you will name him Jesus. He will be the king over all of Israel, and his kingdom will never end." Mary was puzzled by Gabriel's message since she and Joseph were not yet married. Gabriel told her she would have the baby by the power of God. Then Mary said, "I am the Lord's servant, and I am willing to do what he wants. May everything you say come true!"

JULY 15

ZECHARIAH WAS a priest in the temple at Jerusalem. He and his wife, Elizabeth, were sad because they thought they were too old to have children.

One day the angel Gabriel visited Zechariah. "God is going to send a baby son to you and your wife," Gabriel said, "You shall call him John."

"How can I be sure this is true?" Zechariah asked, very surprised.

"Because you don't believe my words from God," Gabriel said, "you won't be able to talk until the baby is born." And sure enough, after the angel left Zechariah discovered that he couldn't speak!

JULY 16

JOSEPH WAS A KIND man who loved God. He also loved Mary and wanted to marry her, so he was sad when he found out she was going to have a baby. He didn't understand who the baby's father was. Then one night God sent an angel to Joseph in a dream. The angel told Joseph he should go ahead with his plans for Mary to be his wife. Then the angel said her baby was going to be born because of God's Holy Spirit. God wanted Joseph to take care of Mary and the baby.

207

JULY 17

A FEW DAYS after the angel Gabriel told Mary she was going to have a baby, Mary went to visit her cousin, Elizabeth. Even though Elizabeth was very old, she was going to have a baby too. Elizabeth gave Mary a big hug! She knew without Mary telling her that Mary was going to have a baby. And she also knew the baby would be God's very own Son! Mary was happy and full of thanks to God. She stayed with Elizabeth for a few months before going back home to Nazareth.

July 18

ELIZABETH WAS SO HAPPY that she was finally going to have a baby! When her baby was born, everyone thought he'd be called Zechariah, after his father. Instead, Elizabeth said their son would be called John. "But nobody in your family has that name," everyone said. Because Zechariah hadn't believed God about the baby, he hadn't been able to speak for months. But when he wrote the words "His name is John," suddenly Zechariah could talk again! He began to sing and thank God for his goodness.

JULY 19

THE ROMAN GOVERNOR wanted to know how many people were in the Roman Empire. So he told the people they had to travel to their hometowns to be counted. Joseph and Mary had to travel to Bethlehem. It was a long journey on a dry, dusty road. And it was very hard for Mary, who was going to have her baby soon. But because Joseph and Mary obeyed the order, the baby Jesus would be born right where God's prophets in the Old Testament said he would be—in the town of Bethlehem!

JULY 20

AFTER MANY DAYS of
travel, Mary and Joseph arrived in
Bethlehem. The village inn was
full, so they had to stay in a
stable, where the animals slept.
Then Mary's baby boy was born!
She wrapped him in pieces of cloth so he
was warm and comfortable. Then she made a bed
for him by putting straw in a manger, which was
a feedbox for animals. Mary knew this tiny baby was
really the Son of God, the promised Messiah!

211

JULY 21

ON THE NIGHT Jesus was born, some shepherds were watching their sheep in the fields outside Bethlehem. Suddenly the dark sky lit up with a bright light. And right in front of them was an angel! "I bring you good news," said the angel. "The Son of God, the Messiah, has been born tonight! Go to Bethlehem, and you will find him wrapped in cloths and lying in a manger."

JULY 22

THE SHEPHERDS in the fields were amazed. The whole sky was filled with hundreds of angels, praising God. They said, "Glory to God in the highest heaven, and peace on earth!"

When the angels went back to heaven, the shepherds said, "Let's go to Bethlehem! Let's see this wonderful thing that has happened."

They ran to the village and found Mary and Joseph. The baby was lying in a manger, just as the angel said.

The shepherds were so happy! The good news was true—God had sent his Son to earth as a baby!

213

July 23

AS THE SHEPHERDS returned to their fields, they were so happy about what they had seen that night. Even though it was the middle of the night, they ran through the streets of Bethlehem singing and praising God. They didn't keep the good news about the baby a secret. Instead they told everyone they met what the angel had said. The Messiah had been born that very night in Bethlehem.

JULY 24

MARY AND JOSEPH loved their special baby. And they loved God, his Father in heaven. When the baby was eight days old, Mary and Joseph named him Jesus, just as the angel Gabriel had told them to do. Later, they took baby Jesus to the temple in Jerusalem to dedicate him to God. They promised that this special baby would always belong to God!

July 25

WHEN MARY AND JOSEPH took baby Jesus to the temple, they met an old man there named Simeon. Simeon had always loved God. And he'd been waiting for God to send the Messiah, who would save God's people. As soon as Simeon saw baby Jesus, he asked if he could hold the child. "God told me I'd see the Savior of the world before I died," said the old man. "Now I can die a happy man, for I've seen him!"

JULY 26

AN OLD WOMAN named Anna was also at the temple when Mary and Joseph came with baby Jesus. She had been a prophet for many years. She was always praying and singing songs to God. When Anna saw the baby Jesus with Simeon, she knew just how special he was. She thanked God for him. Then she talked to everyone who had been waiting for a special King to save them. She said that God's promised Savior had come at last!

July 27

FAR AWAY, some wise men saw a bright star in the night sky. They believed the star meant an important king had been born. So they traveled to Jerusalem, hoping to find the new king in this big city. Instead they met King Herod, who was very angry to hear that anyone might try to take his power away. He sent the wise men to Bethlehem, where prophets had said the Savior would be born. "When you find the king, tell me where he is so I can worship him too," said Herod. But that wasn't what he really wanted to do. He wanted to kill the little king!

JULY 28

THE WISE MEN FOLLOWED the bright star shining above them until it stopped over a small house in Bethlehem. Inside the house they saw Mary with her son.

They worshiped Jesus and gave him special presents—gold, frankincense, and myrrh. That night God told the wise men in a dream not to return to Jerusalem. So the next day the men went home another way.

JULY 29

LITTLE JESUS wasn't safe in his house in Bethlehem. King Herod knew now that the wise men had gone home without telling him where to find the young king. He was so angry that he gave an order to get rid of every little boy in Bethlehem. So God told Joseph in a dream to leave home right away. That same night Mary and Joseph left for Egypt with Jesus. Later an angel told Joseph that King Herod was dead. Then Joseph and his family were no longer afraid. They traveled back to their own country to live in the town of Nazareth.

JULY 30

WHEN JESUS WAS 12, Joseph and Mary took him to the city of Jerusalem. Each year God's people went to the temple there for the Passover. They went to remember how God had saved his people who lived long ago. When it was time to return home, the streets of Jerusalem were crowded. Mary and Joseph thought Jesus was with family or friends. When they learned he was missing, they hurried back to the city. After three days they found him at the temple, talking with the teachers. All who heard him were amazed at how much he knew. And everyone loved him.

July 31

JOHN, THE SON of Zechariah and Elizabeth, was just a few months older than Jesus. When John grew up, he lived in the desert. His clothes were made from scratchy camel's hair, and he ate locusts and honey. God gave him important words to say, and people came from all over to listen to him. John told them, "Tell God you are sorry for the wrong things you do. Start over again. Live good lives that please God, because God's kingdom is on its way." Because of his words, many people asked God to forgive them. John baptized these people in the Jordan River to show they now had a new life.

AUGUST 1

SOME PEOPLE who came to hear John preaching in the desert began to wonder if John was the Savior God had promised. "No!" said John. "Someone who is much greater than I am will come. I'm just helping everyone get ready for him." One day Jesus asked John to baptize him in the Jordan River. When Jesus came up out of the water, God's Holy Spirit came down from the heavens as a dove and rested on Jesus! Then God spoke from heaven. "You are my dear Son," he told Jesus. "I love you, and I'm very pleased with you."

AUGUST 2

AFTER JESUS WAS BAPTIZED, he went into the desert for 40 days and nights. He ate nothing all that time and was very hungry. Satan tried to make Jesus do

wrong things. But each time, Jesus said, "No!" First Satan told Jesus to turn stones into bread. Jesus wouldn't do it. Then Satan promised Jesus the whole world. "Just worship me instead of God," Satan said. But Jesus refused. So Satan told Jesus to jump off the top of the temple, saying, "God will send angels to save you!" But Jesus wouldn't do it. He knew it would be wrong to test God. Finally Satan gave up and went away.

AUGUST 3

JESUS LEFT THE desert and begun teaching people about God. He went from town to town, and everyone who heard him thought well of him. Then Jesus went back to Nazareth, his hometown. He spoke in the synagogue, where people came to pray. The people were amazed by his words. "How can this be Joseph's son?" they asked. Many people became angry when Jesus said he was God's Son. They drove him out of town and even wanted to kill him. But God kept Jesus safe and helped him get away.

AUGUST 4

ONE DAY JESUS walked by and saw John the Baptist talking with two of his followers. John had baptized Jesus the day before, so he said, "This is God's Son." He didn't mind when the men left to follow Jesus. That evening one of the men, Andrew, ran to find his brother, Simon. "Come and meet the Savior!" Andrew said. Jesus gave Simon a new name—Peter, which means "rock." Jesus knew someday Peter would be strong, like a rock.

AUGUST 5

THE NEXT DAY Jesus wanted to go to the town of Galilee. He found a man named Philip and asked him to follow him and be one of his disciples. First Philip went to find his friend Nathanael. "I have found the person Moses and the prophets wrote about!" said Philip. "His name is Jesus, and he's the son of Joseph from Nazareth."

Nathanael rolled his eyes. "Can anything good come from that town?" he asked.

"Come and see," said Philip.

When he met Jesus, Nathanael found out Jesus already knew all about him. Then Nathanael believed Jesus really was God's Son!

227

AUGUST 6

JESUS WENT TO a wedding in the town of Cana with his mother, Mary, and his disciples. The party was going well until the wine ran out. Mary asked Jesus to help. Then she told the servants to do whatever he said. Jesus told them to fill some large stone jars with water and dip into them. When the servants did, the water had turned to wine! And it was even better than the wine they had been serving. When the disciples saw this miracle, they believed that Jesus really was God's Son!

AUGUST 7

A JEWISH LEADER named Nicodemus heard about the wonderful things Jesus was doing. He wanted to meet Jesus because he knew God had sent him. But he was afraid to let anyone see him with Jesus. So he met Jesus when it was dark. Jesus told Nicodemus how he could be in God's kingdom. "You must be born again. You need God's Holy Spirit to give you new life."

"What do you mean?" Nicodemus asked.

"God loves everyone in this world so much that he sent his only Son," Jesus said. "Everyone who believes in him will live with God— forever!"

AUGUST 8

JESUS AND HIS disciples were traveling through Samaria. The hot sun made them very thirsty. When they came to a well, the disciples said to Jesus, "Rest by this well, and we'll go find some food." As Jesus waited, a woman came to get water from the well. Jesus asked her for a drink. The woman was surprised that Jesus asked her for water, because Jews usually didn't talk to Samaritans. "If you knew who I was," said Jesus, "you would ask me for a drink. I can give you water that brings life—life that lasts forever!"

AUGUST 9

THE WOMAN AT THE WELL wanted to know more about the special kind of water Jesus told her about. "Where can you get this water that gives life that will last forever?" she asked.

"If you drink it once," Jesus said, "you'll never be thirsty again."

When Jesus seemed to know everything about her life, she was very surprised. She ran to tell her friends. "Come and meet a man who told me everything I've done. Maybe he's the Savior we've been waiting for!" Many people followed her back to the well. And soon they all believed Jesus was the Savior sent by God.

AUGUST 10

JESUS TAUGHT many people by the Sea of Galilee. One day Jesus got into Peter's boat, and Peter pushed the boat into the water so the people by the side of the lake could see and hear Jesus. When he was done talking, Jesus told Peter to throw his nets into the water. "We fished all night and didn't catch a thing," Peter said. But he did what Jesus asked. When the nets filled up with fish and began to break, Peter fell down on his knees. He was completely amazed. "Don't be afraid," Jesus said. "From now on you'll be fishing for people!"

AUGUST 11

MATTHEW WAS a tax collector. He took people's money and kept some of it for himself. One day Jesus saw Matthew. "Follow me," Jesus said. Immediately the tax collector left everything to follow Jesus. Being one of Jesus' followers made Matthew happy. So he had a party for Jesus and invited his friends. But when the Jewish teachers saw Jesus at the party, they were upset. "Why are you with these dishonest people?" they asked Jesus.

"I'm here to help people who need me," Jesus said. "And people who do what's wrong are the ones who need me most."

233

AUGUST 12

JESUS TRAVELED to Capernaum in Galilee. One day the synagogue was full because everyone came to hear Jesus talk about God. But there was a man in the crowd who couldn't listen quietly. An evil spirit controlled him. The man jumped up and shouted, "What do you want, Jesus? I know you are God's Holy One!"

Jesus told the evil spirit to be quiet and come out of the man. The evil spirit threw the man down on the floor as the crowd watched. Then the evil spirit left without hurting him.

The people were amazed to see what Jesus could do!

234

August 13

JESUS WAS WALKING along the lakeshore when he saw two brothers, James and John, who were fishermen. They were throwing their nets into the water. So Jesus called out to them, "Follow me and you'll catch big fish!" Jesus wasn't talking about catching fish in the lake. He was talking about finding people who needed to know about God. The two men dropped their nets and followed Jesus, just like Andrew and Simon Peter. These men were called disciples. Jesus chose 12 disciples to learn from him as he did God's work.

AUGUST 14

JESUS WAS TEACHING the people when a man came up to him and asked for help. The man had painful skin sores. They came from a sickness called leprosy. The man believed Jesus could take away the sores. "I know you can make me well if you want to," the man said, hiding his face.

Jesus reached out and touched the man. "Be healed," Jesus said. And right away the man's sores disappeared! News of Jesus' wonderful power spread quickly. Soon large crowds followed Jesus everywhere.

AUGUST 15

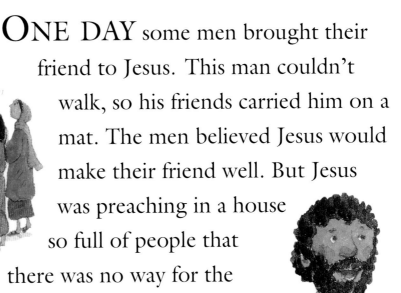

ONE DAY some men brought their friend to Jesus. This man couldn't walk, so his friends carried him on a mat. The men believed Jesus would make their friend well. But Jesus was preaching in a house so full of people that there was no way for the men to get their friend close to Jesus. So they climbed some outside steps to the flat roof. Then they made a large hole in the roof and lowered their friend down to Jesus! When he saw how much the men believed in him, Jesus said to their friend, "Your sins are forgiven." To prove he had the power to forgive the man's sins, Jesus told him to get up, and he did! The man jumped up and ran home, singing his thanks to God.

AUGUST 16

THERE WAS a special pool just inside the city of Jerusalem. Sick people would lie around this pool, waiting for the water to move. They believed that the first one to get into the water after it was stirred up would get well.

One man lying there had been sick for 38 years.

Jesus asked him, "Do you really want to get well?"

"Of course!" the man said. "But I have no one to help me get into the pool."

"Then get up now!" Jesus said. "Pick up your mat and walk."

And the man did! He rolled up his mat and began to walk!

AUGUST 17

ONE EVENING Jesus' disciples climbed into a small boat. They began rowing across the Lake of Galilee toward a town on the other side of the water. But as they rowed, the clouds grew dark. The wind became strong. Huge waves rocked the boat back and forth. Then the disciples saw someone walking toward them—on top of the water!

Their hearts began to pound. But then a voice called out, "It's me. Jesus. Don't be afraid."

When Jesus climbed into the boat, the disciples were surprised to find out they were already on the other side of the lake. Jesus had kept them safe in the storm.

AUGUST 18

JESUS TRAVELED all over the country with his disciples. He healed many people. Soon more people began bringing their sick friends and family to Jesus.

One man who had an evil spirit that kept him from being able to say anything was brought to Jesus. But Jesus was stronger than the evil spirit. Jesus told the evil spirit to leave the man, and the man was healed!

Many people saw what Jesus did and were amazed. "Nothing this wonderful has ever happened in Israel!" they said.

AUGUST 19

THE SABBATH was a special day for God's people to worship him. One Sabbath Jesus met a man with a deformed hand. Some Jewish leaders asked, "Is it right to heal on the Sabbath?"

Jesus answered them with another question. "Would you save your sheep if it fell into a well on the Sabbath?" Everyone was quiet. "People are more important than sheep," Jesus said. "So it's right to do good on the Sabbath." Then Jesus told the man to hold out his hand. When he did, the man's hand became normal, and he could use it!

AUGUST 20

JESUS OFTEN SURPRISED people by the things he said. One day Jesus was teaching about love. "It's easy to love people if they love you," he said. "Everyone does that. Even people who do bad things are kind to people who are kind to them. But you must also love your enemies, no matter what they do to you. Pray for them and help them. Don't even think about whether they will help you back. Just remember to always treat others the way you want them to treat you. Be loving and kind—just like God."

AUGUST 21

JESUS LOVED to tell stories. They helped people understand his teachings. One day he told this story. "Once a wise man built his house on a rock. This house was so strong that nothing could make it fall down. A storm came, and then a flood. But the house stood strong. People who obey me are like the man who built that house—solid as a rock." Then he told another story. "A foolish man built his house on the sand. When the rain came down and the floodwaters rose, the house fell flat. If you hear what I say but don't do what I tell you, you're like the man whose house fell apart."

AUGUST 22

ONE DAY some Jewish leaders told Jesus, "An important officer in the Roman army needs your help. He's worried about his servant, who is very sick." So Jesus left to go to the officer's house. When he was almost there, some of the officer's friends met him. "Our friend feels he's not good enough to have you visit. But he believes that if you give the order, his servant will be well. He believes you have control over sickness just as he has control over his soldiers."

Jesus was happy that the officer believed in him. When the men saw the officer's servant again, he was well!

AUGUST 23

JESUS AND HIS FRIENDS stopped in the town of Nain. They met some people carrying the body of a young man. His mother was crying. Her husband had died and now her only son had died too. Jesus felt very sad for her. Then he went over to the young man's body. "Get up, young man!" he said. And the young

man sat up! With tears in her eyes, the woman hugged her son. The people knew that only God, working through Jesus, could have done such a wonderful thing.

AUGUST 24

JOHN THE BAPTIST

sent his followers to ask Jesus if he was the Messiah, the one God had chosen to be the Savior of the world. Jesus told them, "Just think about all the wonderful things I've done, and you'll know the answer to your question. I've made sick people well. I've brought dead people back to life. And I've preached good news to poor people."

When John's friends left, Jesus turned to the people with him. "John is the greatest man who has ever lived," he said. "God sent him to prepare the way for me."

AUGUST 25

JOHN ALWAYS TOLD the truth, even when it put him in danger. He told King Herod it was wrong for him to marry his brother's wife. This made the king and queen so angry that they threw John into prison.

One day, at a birthday party for the king, the queen's daughter danced for everyone. The king was so pleased with her dance that he promised her anything she wanted. The queen told her to ask the king to have John the Baptist killed. The king was sorry, but he couldn't break his promise. So he gave the order for John to be killed.

247

AUGUST 26

JESUS WAS INVITED to the home of a Jewish leader named Simon. While he was there, a woman poured perfume on Jesus' feet. Simon thought Jesus should push her away because she'd done many wrong things. So Jesus asked Simon to think about two people who owed a man money. "One owed 500 coins, and the other owed just 50. Which of them will love the man most if he doesn't make them pay him back?" Simon said, "The one who owed the most money." Jesus said, "This woman had many sins that have been forgiven and forgotten. That's why she has shown more love to me than you have."

AUGUST 27

JESUS TOLD A STORY about a farmer. "The farmer sowed some seeds. A few seeds fell on a path where birds ate them. Some seeds fell on stones or weeds, which kept them from growing. But some seeds fell on good soil and grew into healthy plants." Then Jesus explained the story. "Some people don't believe anything they hear about God—they are like the seeds the birds ate. Others believe until troubles come. Then they don't practice what they have learned. They are like the seeds among stones and weeds. But people who listen and learn from God are like the seeds that fell on good soil."

AUGUST 28

JESUS TOLD MANY STORIES to teach everyone about his Father's kingdom in heaven. These stories are called parables.

In one story, Jesus told about a man who found a treasure buried in a field. The man was so happy that he sold everything he owned just to be able to buy the field and own the treasure. Jesus wanted his friends to know that God's kingdom is like a valuable treasure.

AUGUST 29

THE DISCIPLES listened as Jesus told them another story about the kingdom of heaven. "A rich man had been buying and selling the best pearls all his life," Jesus said. "One day he came across a pearl that was bigger and better and worth more than any other pearl he'd ever seen! It was beautiful and perfect in every way. The man knew right away that he had to have this pearl. Nothing else mattered anymore. He sold everything he had—even his fine clothes and his home—to buy that one wonderful pearl. That's how special the kingdom of heaven is."

AUGUST 30

ONE DAY JESUS AND HIS FRIENDS got into a boat and began to sail across the lake. On the way across the lake, Jesus lay down for a nap.

While he was sleeping, a great storm came up. "Wake up!" the disciples shouted. "We're going to drown!"

Jesus stood up and told the wind and waves to be still—and they were!

Then Jesus asked his disciples, "Why didn't you trust me to keep you safe?"

AUGUST 31

AFTER THE STORM ended, Jesus arrived on land. A man who was full of evil spirits ran toward him, screaming and shouting. "Leave me alone!" he cried. "I know you are the Son of God!" Jesus ordered the spirits to come out of the man. So the spirits went into some pigs nearby. The pigs ran down a hill and into the lake, where they drowned. The owners of the pigs hurried into town and told everyone what Jesus had done for the wild man. Many people came to see the man, who was now sitting quietly with Jesus.

The man wanted to leave home and follow Jesus, but Jesus asked him to stay where he was. "Tell everyone here what I have done for you," Jesus said.

253

SEPTEMBER 1

PEOPLE PUSHED and shoved as a crowd gathered to see Jesus. Everyone wanted to see this wonderful teacher. As Jesus made his way through the crowd, he stopped and asked, "Who touched me?" Peter, one of Jesus' disciples, thought this was a strange question because so many people were pushing against Jesus. Then a woman stepped forward. She said, "I was the one. I've been sick for 12 years. I knew if I just touched your coat, I would get better. Now I'm well again." Jesus smiled. "You believed in me," he told her. "And that's why you are well."

SEPTEMBER 2

A MAN NAMED JAIRUS was afraid. His only child was so sick that she was going to die. She was just 12 years old. Jairus ran to find Jesus to ask him to save his daughter's life. So Jesus followed Jairus back to his house. But on the way, someone told them the little girl had died. "Don't be afraid," Jesus said to the sad father. "Just trust me to help your daughter, and she'll be all right."

When they came into Jairus' house, Jesus said, "She's not dead. She's only sleeping. Little girl, get up." And she got up right away! Then Jesus told her happy parents to give her something to eat.

SEPTEMBER 3

TWO BLIND MEN followed Jesus along the road. They began shouting for Jesus to help them. Jesus kept going until he got to the house where he was staying. But the men wanted his help so much that they followed Jesus inside! Jesus asked them if they really believed he could help them see. "Yes, Lord," they answered. Jesus touched their eyes. "Because you believe in me, you will see," he told them. Suddenly the men could see! Jesus told them not to say anything, but they couldn't keep the good news to themselves. Everywhere they went, they told people about Jesus.

SEPTEMBER 4

WHEN JESUS WAS IN THE TEMPLE, he watched as the crowds put their gifts into the collection box. Many rich people put in large amounts of money.

Then a poor widow came by and dropped in two pennies. "This poor widow has given more than all the others have given," Jesus said. "They gave just a little bit of what they have. She is poor, but she gave everything she has."

257

SEPTEMBER 5

JESUS GAVE HIS DISCIPLES the power to do the same miracles he'd been doing. This power came from God, his Father in heaven. Then Jesus sent them out to tell everyone about the kingdom of God and to heal the sick. "Don't take any clothes or food or money," Jesus said. "When you enter a village, be a guest in only one home. If the people won't accept your message, shake the dust off your feet as you leave. It will be a sign that you have given up on that village." So the disciples went out to teach people about God and to make sick people well.

SEPTEMBER 6

CROWDS OF PEOPLE found Jesus wherever he went. And Jesus always told them about God. He made sick people well too. One day over 5,000 people were listening to Jesus. They were getting hungry. But no one had any food except for one boy, who had a lunch of five loaves of bread and two fish. Jesus took the lunch and thanked God for it. When he told his disciples to share the food, there was enough to feed everyone! And there were even 12 baskets of food left over!

SEPTEMBER 7

A WOMAN from another country begged Jesus for help. "My daughter has an evil spirit!" she cried. The disciples wanted to send the woman away. But Jesus told the woman, "I have come only to help God's people." The woman wouldn't give up. "Even dogs eat the scraps of food that fall from the table," she said. When Jesus saw that the woman believed in him, he said, "You have great faith. I will give you what you want." Right then the evil spirit left, and her daughter was well again!

SEPTEMBER 8

JESUS SPENT LOTS of time alone praying to God. One day, after he had been by himself, he came to his disciples and asked them, "Who do people say I am?"

They answered, "Some people say you are John the Baptist. Some think you are Elijah. And others think you are one of the other ancient prophets risen from the dead."

Then Jesus asked his disciples who they thought he was. Peter was the first to answer. "You are the Messiah sent to us from God!" he said.

SEPTEMBER 9

JESUS TOOK Peter, James, and John to the top of a mountain to pray. But the three disciples quickly fell asleep. While they slept, Jesus began to pray. Suddenly a bright light woke the disciples up. They saw that Jesus' face was shining, and his clothes were as bright as the sun. The next thing they knew, Moses and Elijah—leaders from long ago—were standing with Jesus. Then a cloud came over them and a voice said, "This is my Son, my chosen one. You must listen to him."

SEPTEMBER 10

A BIG CROWD met Jesus and his friends Peter, James, and John when they came back down from the mountain. A man from the crowd begged Jesus to help his child, saying, "He's my only child, and an evil spirit won't leave him alone. I asked your disciples to send the evil spirit away, but they couldn't." Jesus told the man to go and get his son. As they were coming toward Jesus, the evil spirit threw the boy to the ground. But when Jesus ordered the evil spirit to leave the boy, it did! The boy was all right again. Everyone who saw this was amazed. They knew only God's power could have helped Jesus make the boy well again.

SEPTEMBER 11

ONE DAY JESUS' DISCIPLES began to fight about which one of them was the greatest. They all believed Jesus would soon be king. And each one thought he should have the best job in Jesus' kingdom. Jesus knew what his friends were thinking. So he asked a small child to come over to him.

"God doesn't think about greatness in the same way you do," Jesus said. "Look at this child. You may not think he's very important. But if you welcome him, you welcome me and also my Father. In God's kingdom, the person you think is the least important is really the most important of all!"

SEPTEMBER 12

ON THE WAY to Jerusalem Jesus met a man who wanted to follow him. Jesus told the man it wouldn't be easy, so the man left. Later Jesus asked another man to come with him. But the man said he had to take care of things at home first. "Preaching about God's kingdom is more important than anything," Jesus said. A third man didn't want to follow Jesus until he'd said good-bye to his family. Jesus knew the man wasn't ready to follow him. "You must look forward, not backward, when you follow God," said Jesus.

265

SEPTEMBER 13

JESUS TOLD Peter a story about forgiving people. "A servant owed the king a lot of money, which he couldn't pay. So the king told him, 'Then your whole family must be sold as slaves.' The servant begged the king for mercy. So the king said, 'All right. You don't have to pay back any money. I forgive you everything!'

Later the servant met a friend who owed him just a little money. When the friend couldn't pay, the servant had him thrown in jail. The king was angry when he heard about this. 'You should have forgiven your friend just as I forgave you,' the king said. Then he made his servant pay back every penny he owed."

SEPTEMBER 14

TO HELP PEOPLE understand the kingdom of heaven, Jesus told this story. "Early one morning, a farmer offered to pay some workers for a day's work. Later he hired more workers. In the evening he hired even more. At the end of the day the farmer paid each worker the same. 'That's not fair!' said those who had worked all day. The farmer told them he was kind to all the workers no matter how long they worked." Then Jesus said, "In my Father's kingdom, those who seem to be first will really be last. And those who are last now will have first place in the kingdom someday."

SEPTEMBER 15

A JEWISH TEACHER asked Jesus how to have life that lasts forever. "What do God's laws say?" Jesus asked.

"Love God and love your neighbor," the man answered.

So Jesus told a story about who our neighbors are. "A man was hurt by robbers and left for dead. A priest and another leader came by, but they didn't stop to help. Then a Samaritan, who was from another country, came along. He gave the man the help he needed. That means," Jesus said, "that you must be a good neighbor and show love to everyone, just like the good Samaritan did."

SEPTEMBER 16

MARY AND MARTHA were sisters who were good friends of Jesus. They lived in the small town of Bethany, not far from Jerusalem. One day Jesus went to see them on his way to the city. As soon as he came to the door, Mary stopped everything she was doing and sat down to talk with Jesus. But Martha kept rushing around getting the meal ready. Martha soon got angry with her sister. "Can't you tell Mary to help me in the kitchen?" she asked Jesus. But Jesus said, "Martha, you are so upset about all these details! Mary has chosen to spend time with me," he said. "That's the most important thing of all."

269

SEPTEMBER 17

JESUS WENT OFF by himself to pray. When he had finished, one of his disciples said, "Teach us how to pray."

So Jesus told them, "Begin your prayers by honoring God the Father. Then ask for God's kingdom to come soon. Also think about the things you need. Ask God to give you food for each day. And ask him to forgive you for the wrong things you do, just as you forgive people who hurt or upset you. And then ask God to keep you from sinning again."

This prayer that Jesus taught his disciples is now called "The Lord's Prayer."

270

SEPTEMBER 18

JESUS WANTED HIS DISCIPLES to know that God would answer their prayers. "Think about a friend coming to visit you at midnight," Jesus said. "You have no food in the house, so you run to your neighbor's house and knock on the door. 'Please let me borrow some bread,' you say. Because it's so late, your neighbor doesn't want to help, even though you are friends. But he gets up and gives you some bread, because he knows you won't stop bothering him until he does." Then Jesus said, "If you ask God for some-thing, he'll give it to you. It's like knocking on a door and having it open for you."

SEPTEMBER 19

ONE DAY A MAN asked Jesus for help. "My father has died, and my brother won't share our family's things," he said.

"There are more important things to think about," Jesus said. Then he told a story. "A farmer grew so much grain that he filled his barns. So he built a bigger barn. 'Now I can eat, drink, and be happy,' he said. But God asked him, 'Can you take any of this with you when you die? Tonight your life will end.'" Then Jesus said, "Don't be greedy for what you don't have. Real life is not about how much you own."

SEPTEMBER 20

"DON'T WORRY about where your next meal will come from," Jesus told his disciples. "And don't worry about what to wear. Life is about much more than food and clothes. Look at the birds. God gives them food to eat. But you are worth much more to God than birds. Look at the flowers in the fields. God made them more beautiful than the fine clothes kings wear. If you obey God, he'll make sure you have everything you need."

SEPTEMBER 21

ON THE SABBATH everyone rested and took time to worship God together. It was against the Jewish law to do any work on this day. One Sabbath Jesus met a woman in the synagogue. She hadn't been able to stand up straight for 18 years. Jesus felt sorry for the hurting woman, so he made her well. She could stand straight again! But one of the Jewish leaders told Jesus, "You shouldn't make people well on the Sabbath. That's working." Jesus answered, "But you untie your donkey to give it water on the Sabbath. So why shouldn't I help this woman?"

The synagogue leader couldn't think of an answer to give Jesus.

SEPTEMBER 22

THE JEWISH RULERS were proud of their riches. Jesus told them a story about a very rich man who had everything he could possibly want. A poor, starving beggar named Lazarus lay at his gate, begging for scraps of food. Finally, lonely and sick, the beggar died. Angels carried him to heaven to be with Abraham. When the rich man died, he went to the place of the dead. He could see the beggar in heaven, happy and comfortable. The rich man begged Abraham to send Lazarus to help him. But Abraham said, "You had everything when you were on earth, but Lazarus had nothing. Now he is being comforted!"

275

SEPTEMBER 23

JESUS MET A BEGGAR who had been born blind. Jesus' disciples asked, "Is this man blind because his parents did things that were wrong? Or did the blind man do things that were wrong?"

Jesus answered, "The man isn't blind because of anything bad he or his family did. This man is blind so that people will see the power of God at work." Then Jesus spit on the ground. He made some mud and gently covered the man's eyes with it. "Wash in that pool over there," Jesus said. So the man washed off the mud, and came back seeing—for the first time ever!

SEPTEMBER 24

JESUS TOLD his followers, "A hired helper might run away if he sees a wolf coming. He might let the wolf attack the sheep because he isn't their shepherd. He doesn't really care about them. But I am the good shepherd. I know my own sheep, and they know me. And I would lay down my life for my sheep. My sheep recognize my voice. I know them, and they follow me."

SEPTEMBER 25

MANY PEOPLE were wondering about God's kingdom. Could only certain people could be in it? Could any of them be a part of it?

"I'll tell you what God's kingdom is like," Jesus said. "A man asked his friends to come to a dinner party. But on the day of the party, they all said they couldn't come. So the man told his servant, 'Go into town. Ask poor people and people who can't walk or see to come to my party. Because the people I asked first didn't come to my party, they won't get even one little taste of what I had for them!'"

SEPTEMBER 26

GREAT CROWDS WERE following Jesus. He told them, "If you want to follow me, you must love me more than your family—even more than your own life."

He explained, "You don't start building something until you know how much it will cost. That way you know for sure you won't run out of money. And a king doesn't begin a war unless he knows he has enough soldiers to win. So no one can be my disciple without giving up everything for me."

SEPTEMBER 27

SOME IMPORTANT JEWISH

leaders were complaining that Jesus made friends with sinners— people they believed did bad things. Jesus knew what the leaders were saying about him.

So he told them, "If you had 100 sheep and one of them got lost, wouldn't you leave the rest to go and look for the missing sheep? And when you found it, you would celebrate, wouldn't you? Well, there is more joy in heaven about one sinner who is sorry than about 99 good people who don't need to say they're sorry."

SEPTEMBER 28

BEFORE THE JEWISH LEADERS could say anything about the lost-sheep story, Jesus told another story. "There was a woman who had ten very special silver coins. One day she lost one of them. So she looked all over her house from top to bottom for the missing coin. After a long time, she saw something bright and shiny in a dark corner. It was the lost coin! She was so happy that she went to tell her friends the good news." Jesus paused, then said, "This is what it is like in heaven when one lost sinner is sorry and comes back to God."

SEPTEMBER 29

JESUS TOLD another story about a man with two sons. The younger son asked for his share of the family's money, so his father gave it to him. Then this son left home. He went far away and lived a wild life, using up the money in a hurry. He soon had no money left for food, and he began to starve. Finally the young man got a job feeding pigs. He was so hungry even the pigs' food looked good to him! Then he said to himself, "Even my father's servants have more to eat than I do. I'll go back home and ask my father to forgive me. Perhaps he'll let me work for him."

September 30

As soon as the father saw the young man, he ran out to hug him! The son said, "I've sinned, and now I don't deserve to be called your son." But his father gave the son his finest robe to wear, along with a ring for his finger and new sandals. The father threw a big party for his son. But the older brother was angry because his father never gave him anything, even though he had always been obedient. "Everything I have is also yours, my son," the father told him. "But we had to celebrate this happy day. The son I thought was dead is alive!"

OCTOBER 1

JESUS' FRIEND Lazarus was very sick. His sisters, Mary and Martha, sent a message to Jesus, asking him to come right away. But Jesus stayed where he was for two more days, teaching his followers and making people well. Then Jesus told his disciples it was time to leave for Lazarus' house. "My friend has gone to sleep, and I must wake him up now," Jesus told them. He knew they thought Lazarus must have been getting better. So he said, "In fact, Lazarus has already died. But when you see what I am about to do, that will help you believe in me."

OCTOBER 2

WHEN JESUS CAME to Lazarus' house, Martha ran to meet him. "If you had come sooner, you could have saved my brother from dying!" she cried. Jesus said to her, "I bring new life that lasts forever. People who believe in me will live again, even after they have died." But when Jesus saw how sad Mary was, he cried too. Together they all went to Lazarus' tomb. "Roll back the stone!" Jesus ordered. Then he said, "Lazarus, come out." And Lazarus walked right out into the sunlight! Friends took off the cloths that had been wrapped around Lazarus' body. And many people believed in Jesus because of this amazing miracle.

OCTOBER 3

JESUS WAS ON HIS WAY to Jerusalem when he stopped at a small village. Ten men called out, "Please, Jesus, help us." These men had sores from leprosy all over their skin. They had to live outside the village, away from their families.

"Find a priest in the village, and show him you're well," Jesus told the men. They did as Jesus said. And on their way into town, all their sores went away!

But only one of the men came back to thank Jesus.

"Where are the others?" Jesus asked. "Didn't I heal 10 men? You can stand up and go now. You're well because you believed in me."

OCTOBER 4

JESUS TOLD A STORY to teach people that no one is more important than anyone else. He said, "Two men went to the temple. One was a Jewish leader, and the other was a dishonest tax collector. The leader stood up and prayed in a loud voice, 'Thank you, God, that I never do things that are wrong like that man over there.'

"But the tax collector looked down and prayed quietly, 'Forgive me, God, for the wrong things I've done.'

"God answered the tax collector's prayer," Jesus said, "but he didn't listen to the proud leader."

OCTOBER 5

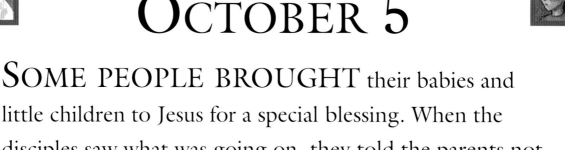

SOME PEOPLE BROUGHT their babies and little children to Jesus for a special blessing. When the disciples saw what was going on, they told the parents not to bother Jesus. They thought he had more important work to do. But Jesus gathered the children around himself. "Let the children come to me. Don't try to stop them!" he told his disciples. "God's kingdom belongs to little ones like these. To get into the kingdom of God, everyone must love and trust me the way these little children do."

OCTOBER 6

A RICH YOUNG MAN asked Jesus what he must do to live forever. "You must obey God's laws," Jesus said. " 'Don't kill. Don't steal. Don't tell lies. Be kind to your father and mother.' "

"I've obeyed those since I was a boy," said the man. "Now give all your money to help the poor. Then come, follow me," Jesus said. This made the man sad. He didn't want to give up his money, so he walked away from Jesus. Then Jesus said to his disciples, "It's very hard for rich people to get into God's kingdom."

OCTOBER 7

A BLIND BEGGAR named Bartimaeus sat by the road outside Jericho. Suddenly he heard people talking close by. "Jesus is coming this way," someone told him. So Bartimaeus began to shout for Jesus' help.

When people told Bartimaeus to be quiet, he shouted more. Jesus stopped and asked him, "What do you want me to do for you?"

"I want to see!" he said.

"Because you believe in me you can see!" said Jesus. Then the man could see, and he followed Jesus, thanking God.

OCTOBER 8

LARGE CROWDS waited in Jericho to see Jesus. One very short man, a tax collector named Zacchaeus, couldn't see over the other people, so he climbed a tree. Jesus looked up at him. "Hurry down," said Jesus. "I'm coming to your house today." After he met Jesus, Zacchaeus wanted to obey God. He gave half his money to the poor. And he gave back tax money than he'd stolen from others! Jesus said, "This is why I am here—to find those who have lost their way and bring them back to God."

OCTOBER 9

JESUS TOLD THIS STORY about how to live wisely while waiting for the kingdom of God to come. "A rich master went on a trip. But first he gave each of his servants 10 coins. When he returned, the first servant said, 'My coins are worth 10 times more.' The second servant said, 'My coins are worth five times more.' The rich man was happy with these servants. But another servant said, 'I hid your coins to keep them safe. They're worth nothing more now than they were before.' The master was angry. 'This man has done nothing for me,' he said, 'so I'll take away the little he has. I'll give his coins to the one who did the most for me.' "

OCTOBER 10

MARY AND HER SISTER, Martha, were thankful that Jesus had brought their brother, Lazarus, back to life. One day Jesus was at a dinner party at their house. While Martha served the food, Mary opened a jar of expensive perfume. And she poured it over Jesus' feet to show her love for him. Judas Iscariot, one of Jesus' disciples, saw what Mary did and got angry. "You could have sold your perfume and given the money to poor people," he said. But Jesus told him to leave Mary alone. He knew Judas only wanted the money for himself. Then Jesus said, "Poor people will always be here for you to help. But I won't be with you for much longer."

293

OCTOBER 11

JESUS SENT two disciples into a small town near Jerusalem. "Find a young donkey that no one has ever ridden and bring it to me," he said. So the disciples found the donkey and told the owners that Jesus needed it. Then the two men brought the donkey to Jesus so he could ride it into Jerusalem.

The crowds spread their coats on the road ahead of Jesus. His followers began waving palm branches and singing, "God bless the king, who comes in the name of the Lord."

OCTOBER 12

JESUS KNEW he was going to leave his disciples soon. But he wanted them to understand that he was coming back. So he said, "Think about 10 young women waiting for the groom to arrive for his wedding. Five of them had enough oil to keep their lamps shining all night. The other five didn't bring any oil, and their lamps went out in the middle of the night. So

when the groom came, these five had to go buy oil before they could go to the wedding party. But when they got back, the groom wouldn't open the door because it was too late." Jesus was saying that everyone should be ready and waiting for his return, even though no one knows exactly when this will be.

OCTOBER 13

ONE DAY JESUS went to the temple in Jerusalem. He was very upset at what he saw. People were buying and selling animals at high prices. This meant that people who had come to worship God were being cheated out of their money. So Jesus began to chase away everyone who was doing the cheating. "It says in the Scriptures that God's house is to be a place of prayer," Jesus said. "But you have made it a place for thieves!" After this he taught about God every day in the temple.

OCTOBER 14

ONE DAY JESUS TOLD told this story. "A man hired some farmers to take care of his grapevines while he was away. Later he sent a servant back to get his share of the grapes. But the farmers beat the servant and didn't give him any grapes. Two more servants were each treated the same way. At last the man said, 'I'll send my son. They'll treat him better.' But the farmers killed the son. So the father killed the farmers and gave his vineyard to other farmers." The temple leaders were angry. They knew Jesus was saying he was the son, and they were the farmers. But soon these very leaders would put Jesus on a cross to die.

297

OCTOBER 15

JESUS TOLD this story to some Jewish leaders. "A man asked one of his sons to help take care of his grapevines for a day. The son said no, but later he changed his mind and helped. The other son said he would help, but then he never did. Which son obeyed his father?" Everyone said the one who helped his father. Then Jesus said, "Some people say no to following God. But later they change their ways and follow him. They are the ones who will be in God's kingdom, not the ones who say they will follow God but are never sorry about the wrong things they do."

OCTOBER 16

JESUS AND HIS DISCIPLES gathered together
to celebrate Passover. Before their meal, Jesus did
something surprising. He poured water into a bowl, got
down on the floor, and began to wash his friends' dirty
feet. He dried them carefully with a towel that was
tied around his waist. "I'm your Lord and teacher,
but you've just seen me wash your feet," Jesus said.
"I've shown you how I want you to act. Do kind,
helpful things for each other, just as
I have done for you."

299

OCTOBER 17

THE 12 DISCIPLES had been with Jesus for three years, learning about God's kingdom. As they sat down to eat the Passover meal together, Jesus told them this was the last supper they would eat together. Then Jesus took some bread and thanked God for it. He broke it into pieces and told his friends the bread was like his body. Next he took a cup of wine and said the wine was like his blood. Jesus was talking about the way he would give up his body and blood when he died on the cross. He would die to save people from their sins.

OCTOBER 18

AFTER THEIR LAST SUPPER

together, Jesus and his disciples went
to the Mount of Olives to pray. Jesus
walked a little way ahead so he could
talk to God alone. "Father," he
prayed, "if you are willing, please
take this suffering away from me. But I

want to do your will, not mine." Jesus was willing to die
on the cross if that's what God wanted.

God helped Jesus by sending an angel to strengthen
him. Then Jesus went to find his disciples. They had gone
to sleep because they were very tired and sad.
"Wake up!" said Jesus. "You
must pray that God will
keep you from
doing wrong."

301

OCTOBER 19

WHILE JESUS WAS talking to his disciples at the Mount of Olives, a group of soldiers arrived. The fire in their torches lit up the dark night. Judas Iscariot, one of Jesus' disciples, walked up to Jesus and greeted him with a kiss. This was a sign to the soldiers that Jesus was the one they wanted to arrest. The soldiers had come with swords and clubs, but Jesus wasn't going to fight. He went with them peacefully.

OCTOBER 20

THE SOLDIERS took Jesus to the house of the high priest. Jesus' disciple Peter followed from a safe distance. He didn't want anyone to know that he was one of Jesus' friends. He joined a group that was keeping warm by a fire outside the high priest's house. Three different people asked Peter if he was Jesus' friend. "No!" said Peter each time. "I don't even know him." Peter was afraid to tell people that Jesus was his best friend and teacher.

OCTOBER 21

AFTER PETER SAID three times that he didn't know Jesus, a rooster crowed. The sun was coming up. All of a sudden Peter felt terrible. He remembered Jesus telling him the night before that Peter would lie three times and say he didn't even know Jesus. Jesus said Peter would do this before the rooster crowed the next morning. Peter hadn't believed Jesus then. But now he knew Jesus was right. Peter was so sorry that he began to cry. And he left the place where Jesus was.

OCTOBER 22

THE SOLDIERS TOOK JESUS to Pilate, the Roman governor. Pilate didn't think that Jesus had done anything wrong. He planned to tell the soldiers to beat Jesus and then let him go. But the crowd yelled loudly, "Crucify him!" They kept shouting that Jesus should be killed, and Pilate finally agreed. He told his soldiers to take Jesus away.

OCTOBER 23

THE SOLDIERS LED JESUS to a place outside Jerusalem called "The Skull." Here people were taken to die when they had done wrong things like stealing and killing. Because the soldiers had beaten Jesus, he was too weak to carry his big wooden cross the whole way. So a man named Simon was told to carry the cross for Jesus. Large crowds followed behind. Many of the women were crying. The soldiers nailed Jesus to the cross and then raised it up high for all to see. Two men hung on a cross, one on each side of Jesus.

OCTOBER 24

JESUS LOOKED down from the cross and prayed, "Father, forgive these people, because they don't know what they're doing." Some of the leaders and soldiers laughed, saying if Jesus were really God, he should save himself. A man on one of the crosses said, "We've done wrong things, but this man hasn't done anything wrong. Remember me, Jesus, when you go to heaven." Jesus told this man, "You'll go with me to heaven today!"

October 25

After Jesus had been

on the cross for a while, the sun stopped shining. It grew very dark, even though it was the middle of the day. And suddenly the thick curtain hanging in the temple was torn into two pieces. Jesus cried out, "Father, I put myself in your hands." Then he died.

The leader of the Roman soldiers saw what happened. He gave thanks to God for Jesus and said, "This was a good man who never did anything wrong." Then many people who were watching went home, crying tears of great sadness.

OCTOBER 26

JOSEPH OF ARIMATHEA was one of the Jewish leaders. But he hadn't wanted to kill Jesus. Bravely, Joseph went to Pilate and asked him for Jesus' body. Pilate said yes. Joseph took Jesus' body to a new tomb, which had been made by cutting into the rock on a hillside. He wrapped Jesus' body in linen cloth and carefully laid it in the tomb. Then he rolled a big stone across the opening of the tomb.

OCTOBER 27

VERY EARLY SUNDAY morning, some women went to the tomb. They brought sweet-smelling spices to put in the tomb. When the women reached the tomb, they found that the stone had been rolled away. They looked inside and saw that Jesus' body was gone!

Then two angels dressed in bright clothes appeared. They had wonderful news. "Jesus is alive again!" they said. The women ran to tell Jesus' disciples what had happened.

OCTOBER 28

WHEN ONE WOMAN, Mary Magdalene, saw that Jesus' body was gone, she began to cry. She saw two angels sitting inside the tomb where Jesus' body had been. "Someone has taken my Lord away," Mary said.

Then Jesus himself came to the garden where the tomb was. But Mary thought he was the gardener. She asked him where Jesus' body was. He said to her, "Mary."

At once, Mary knew that he was Jesus. "Teacher!" she cried. Jesus told Mary to tell the disciples he was returning to his Father in heaven.

311

OCTOBER 29

TWO FOLLOWERS of Jesus were walking back to the village of Emmaus. Jesus came along and began walking beside them. But they didn't know who he was. "What are you talking about? You look so sad," he said.

"Haven't you heard what has happened in the last few days?" they answered. As they walked along, Jesus talked about some things the prophets had written. Then the two men asked Jesus to have supper with them. When Jesus picked up some bread and thanked God for it, the men suddenly knew who he was. They ran back to Jerusalem to tell the disciples!

OCTOBER 30

AFTER JESUS DIED, the disciples always met behind locked doors. They were afraid of the Jewish leaders. The two women told the disciples that they had seen Jesus. Then suddenly Jesus was in the room with them! "Peace be with you," he said. He showed them where his hands and feet had been nailed to the cross. The disciples could hardly believe their eyes! Jesus told them he was sending them out into the world, just as God had sent him. He gave them the Holy Spirit to help them do God's special work.

OCTOBER 31

THOMAS WASN'T with the disciples when Jesus came to them. So he didn't believe that Jesus really was alive again. "I won't believe what you say unless I see Jesus for myself," Thomas said.

A week later the disciples met again in the same house. This time Thomas was there too. As before, suddenly Jesus was in the room! Jesus told Thomas, "Look at the nail marks in my hands, and touch my side where the spear went in. Then believe!" Thomas said to Jesus, "You are my Lord and my God!"

NOVEMBER 1

ONE NIGHT Peter, John, and some other disciples went fishing in a boat. But when the sun began to shine the next morning, their fishing nets were still empty. A man was standing on the shore of the lake. He called to the disciples, "Throw your nets out from the other side of the boat, and you'll get a lot of fish." The men did this, and their nets filled up with so many fish they could hardly pull them into the boat. Then John knew who the man was. "It's the Lord!" he said to Peter. Right away, Peter jumped into the water and swam to Jesus.

315

NOVEMBER 2

THE DISCIPLES who had been fishing with Peter followed him to the shore. Jesus had been frying some fish over a fire. He asked his friends to have breakfast with him. After they ate, Jesus asked Peter, "Do you love me?"

"Yes, Lord, you know I do," said Peter. Jesus asked Peter the same question three times, and each time Peter gave the same answer. Each time Peter answered, Jesus said to him, "Feed my sheep."

Jesus wanted Peter to take care of his followers after Jesus went back to heaven, even when hard times came.

NOVEMBER 3

SOON IT WAS time for Jesus to go back to heaven to be with God. Before he left, he took a group of his followers up on a mountain. He told them to tell people everywhere about him. He said, "Teach these new disciples to obey all the commands I've given you. Baptize them in the name of the Father, Son, and Holy Spirit. And remember, I will always be with you!" Then right before their eyes, Jesus began to go up into the sky. His followers watched him until finally he disappeared into the clouds.

NOVEMBER 4

THE DISCIPLES couldn't forget what they had just seen. One minute Jesus had been talking to them, and then suddenly he went up into the sky! As the disciples stood there looking at the clouds, two men dressed in white came and stood with them. "Why are you looking at the sky?" they asked. "Jesus has gone back to heaven. Someday he will return to earth in the same way you've seen him go."

NOVEMBER 5

THE DISCIPLES

returned to Jerusalem, where they prayed together with thankful hearts. One morning when they were together, a great sound like a strong wind filled the room where they were meeting. A small flame of fire

appeared over each disciple, and they were all filled with the power of the Holy Spirit. Now they could speak in many different languages. People came running to see what was happening. Even people from other countries could understand them! Jesus was now with his disciples in a new and special way. This day was called Pentecost.

NOVEMBER 6

WHEN PEOPLE HEARD the disciples talking in different languages, some of them said the men were drunk. But Peter stood up and told them, "We've been filled with God's Holy Spirit. Remember how you put Jesus on the cross? God brought him back to life so we can be forgiven for our sins."

The people wanted to know what they should do. "Tell God you are sorry for your sins, and be baptized to show that you believe in Jesus," said Peter. "Then the Holy Spirit will come to you, too."

NOVEMBER 7

JESUS' FOLLOWERS didn't always understand the gifts the Holy Spirit sent to them. When a man named Paul became one of Jesus' followers, he wrote other new believers a letter about the gifts of the Holy Spirit.

"The Holy Spirit gives us many gifts," Paul wrote. "Some people have one gift, and other people have other gifts. But the same Holy Spirit gives them all. Some people receive the gift of wisdom, and some get the gift of knowledge. Others have a lot of faith, and still others can heal sick people. Some gifts seem more special than others, but all of them are important to God. These gifts are for everyone who loves Jesus."

November 8

ON THE DAY OF PENTECOST many people turned away from their sins and began to obey Jesus. As Peter preached to the crowd, about three thousand people believed in Jesus in one day! All the new believers wanted to know more about Jesus. So they listened to Peter and the other disciples teach about him. The believers met together to pray and to eat. They sold all their things so they could share their money with the people in their group who were poor and needed help. As the days went by, the number of believers kept getting bigger.

NOVEMBER 9

PETER AND JOHN were on their way to the temple to pray when they saw a man who couldn't walk. Each day his friends carried him to the temple gate, where he begged people for money. Peter said to the man, "I don't have any money for you. But I'll give you what I do have. In the name of Jesus Christ, get up and walk!" Peter took the man's hand and helped him up. The man jumped up, stood on his feet, and began to walk! Then he went into the temple with Peter and John, walking and jumping and praising God.

323

NOVEMBER 10

THE PEOPLE were amazed that Peter healed the crippled man. Peter told them, "The name of Jesus made this man walk!" Because of this, many more people believed in Jesus. This upset the Jewish leaders. They had Peter and John arrested and told them to stop preaching. But Peter and John replied, "We must obey God, not you. We can't stop telling about the great things we've seen and heard!" The Jewish leaders knew that punishing Peter and John would cause a riot, so they let them go free.

NOVEMBER 11

AS SOON AS THEY WERE FREED, Peter and John found the other believers. They told them the Jewish leaders had wanted them to stop preaching about Jesus. All the believers gathered together to pray. They thanked God for his greatness. They prayed that the apostles would be even bolder in their preaching. They asked God to show his amazing power by doing many more miracles. And when the believers finished praying, the whole building where they were meeting shook with the Holy Spirit's power!

325

NOVEMBER 12

SOON THERE were so many new believers that the apostles were spending all their time taking care of them and feeding them! They didn't have enough time for preaching and teaching. So the apostles put seven men in charge of making sure everyone had enough to eat each day. Stephen, one of these men, was very wise and full of God's power. He performed many amazing miracles in Jesus' name. This upset some people who didn't like hearing about Jesus. These people made up lies about Stephen. Then they had him arrested and took him to the Jewish leaders.

NOVEMBER 13

STEPHEN STOOD quietly before the angry Jewish leaders. He knew he had done nothing wrong. Everyone suddenly stopped and looked at Stephen in amazement, because his face began to shine brightly like an angel's! Then it was Stephen's turn to speak. He told everyone how the Jewish people had often turned away from God's chosen leaders. "And now," he said, "you have killed the most important leader of all—God's own Son, Jesus." This made the Jewish leaders even angrier. They dragged Stephen outside the city, where they threw rocks at him. As his enemies stoned him, he asked God to forgive them. Stephen knew he would soon be with Jesus.

327

NOVEMBER 14

AFTER THE JEWISH LEADERS killed Stephen, they wanted to get rid of the rest of Jesus' followers too. A man named Saul looked for believers all over the city. And when he found them, he dragged them from their houses and threw them in jail. The people who believed in Jesus were so afraid that they all left Jerusalem. Only Jesus' disciples stayed.

NOVEMBER 15

JERUSALEM WAS NO longer safe for Jesus' followers, so they all had to leave. But they still talked about Jesus wherever they went. One man, Philip, went to the city of Samaria to tell people about Jesus. The crowds listened carefully to what he said because he also worked many wonderful miracles. Crippled people could suddenly walk. Sick people were healed. There was much joy in Samaria because of Philip's work!

329

NOVEMBER 16

ONE DAY AN angel told Philip to leave Samaria and walk down a lonely desert road. On the road, Philip saw an important Ethiopian leader riding in his carriage. He was reading out loud from the book of the prophet Isaiah.

The Holy Spirit told Philip to walk beside the carriage. So Philip ran over. He heard the man reading from Isaiah's words. Philip asked him if he understood what he was reading. "How can I, when there is no one to teach me?" the man answered. And he begged Philip to come up into his carriage and sit with him.

NOVEMBER 17

PHILIP WAS VERY GLAD to talk with the man from Ethiopia. "Hundreds of years ago, the prophet Isaiah wrote down words that God told him to write," said Philip. "Isaiah wrote about someone who would be killed like an innocent lamb that had done nothing wrong. Those words were really about God's Son, Jesus. Now our sins can be forgiven, because Jesus died for us on the cross and came back to life." When the Ethiopian man saw some water, he asked if he could be baptized. So Philip baptized him. And then the man went on his way, full of joy.

331

NOVEMBER 18

MEANWHILE, SAUL WAS still eager to destroy anyone who believed in Jesus. He traveled to Damascus, planning to arrest Jesus' followers, bring them back to Jerusalem, and put them in jail. Suddenly a bright light from heaven surrounded Saul. It was so bright he fell to the ground. He heard a voice from heaven say, "Saul! Saul! Why are you hurting me?"

"Who are you, sir?" Saul answered.

"I am Jesus," came the answer. "Go on to Damascus, and then I'll tell you what to do." As Saul stood up, he realized he was blind!

NOVEMBER 19

SAUL COULD NO longer see. His friends led him to Damascus, where he stayed three days with no food or water. In a vision, God told a man named Ananias to go to Saul. Ananias was afraid. He'd heard how Saul treated Christians. But God said, "I chose Saul to tell people everywhere about me." Ananias found Saul and put his hands on him. "Saul," he said, "God sent me so you can see again and be filled with the Holy Spirit." Instantly Saul could see, and he was baptized. Now Saul was ready to tell everyone about Jesus.

NOVEMBER 20

SAUL STAYED with the believers in Damascus for a few days. He preached about Jesus to the people there, saying, "He is really the Son of God!" The people were surprised. "Isn't this the same man who hated Jesus and his followers?" they asked. Saul's preaching became more and more powerful. Soon the Jewish leaders decided to kill him. But Saul heard about their plan, and his friends helped him escape. During the night, these friends hid Saul in a basket. They let the basket down through a big hole in the city wall. Then Saul traveled back to Jerusalem.

November 21

WHEN SAUL CAME BACK to Jerusalem, the believers there first thought he was only pretending to believe in Jesus. But one disciple, Barnabas, trusted Saul. He told the other disciples how Saul had met Jesus on the road to Damascus. Then Jesus' disciples accepted Saul. After that he was with them all the time, preaching boldly about Jesus. Soon Saul, who was also called Paul, and Barnabas became great friends. God chose them to go on a special trip to teach more people about Jesus. They sailed away in a boat together, headed for the island of Cyprus.

NOVEMBER 22

PETER, one of Jesus' first disciples, was still telling people about Jesus. He walked from town to town around Jerusalem, preaching to the crowds. Because of Peter, many people became followers of Jesus. While Peter was visiting a town called Lydda, he met a man named Aeneas. Aeneas hadn't been able to walk or even get out of his bed for eight years. "Aeneas," Peter said, "get up and make your bed! Jesus has made you well!" Right away, Aeneas got up and began walking around. Everyone who saw what happened was amazed! And because of this the whole town believed in Jesus.

NOVEMBER 23

A WOMAN NAMED Dorcas lived in the nearby town of Joppa. She was very kind and always helped the poor. While Peter was in Lydda, Dorcas became very ill and died. Her friends ran to Peter, saying, "Please come as soon as you can!" So Peter went to Dorcas's house. He asked everyone to leave the room where Dorcas lay. Then he got down on his knees and prayed. When he turned to Dorcas, he said, "Get up!" And Dorcas opened her eyes. When she saw Peter, she sat up in bed. Dorcas was alive again! Many people in Joppa believed in Jesus after that.

NOVEMBER 24

PETER STAYED FOR a long time in the town of Joppa at the house of a man named Simon. One day while Peter was praying on the flat roof of the house, he saw the sky open up. What looked like a large sheet came down to the ground. Inside the sheet were all sorts of animals that Jewish people had always been told not to eat. Peter heard God's voice saying, "Get up, Peter. Kill and eat them. Everything here is okay for you to eat." Peter was confused. He wondered what God was trying to tell him.

NOVEMBER 25

WHILE PETER WAS still thinking about his vision, three men came to visit him. They worked for Cornelius, a Roman army officer. An angel had told Cornelius to find Peter because Peter would teach him about God. Peter invited his guests to stay overnight. The next day he went with the three men to Cornelius's house. Then Peter finally understood what God had been trying to tell him. Even though Cornelius and his family weren't Jewish, God wanted them to learn about Jesus too. Jesus had come to save everyone, not only the Jews.

NOVEMBER 26

KING HEROD made life hard for the Christians in Jerusalem. He put Peter in jail. Herod would put him on trial after the feast of Passover. Soldiers took turns watching Peter inside the jail. But his friends prayed for him. The night before his trial, Peter was asleep, chained between two soldiers. More soldiers were guarding the prison gate. Suddenly there was a bright light, and an angel stood in front of Peter. "Quick! Get up!" said the angel. At once Peter's chains fell away. "Put your sandals on and come with me," said the angel.

November 27

THE ANGEL LED Peter right past the guards at the prison gate. At first Peter thought he was dreaming. Then the angel left, but Peter knew he was safe! He went to the house where many of the believers were praying together. Peter knocked at the door. A servant girl came to open it. When she heard Peter's voice, she was so happy that she forgot to open the door! She ran back to tell everyone Peter was there. No one believed her, but finally they all went to open the door. They were so surprised! Peter told his friends how God's angel led him out of jail.

NOVEMBER 28

PAUL AND BARNABAS said good-bye to the believers in Jerusalem and sailed on a boat to Cyprus. When they arrived, they visited different places on the island, preaching to the people. The Roman governor of the island sent for Paul and Barnabas because he wanted to hear the word of God. But Elymas, a magician, told the governor not to believe Paul and Barnabas. Paul looked Elymas in the eye and said, "Because you are an enemy of what is good, God will make you blind!" Instantly Elymas was blinded. Because of this the governor believed in Jesus!

NOVEMBER 29

WHEN PAUL AND Barnabas left Cyprus, they sailed to other places. They shared the good news about Jesus with everyone. In the town of Lystra, they met a man with crippled feet. He listened closely to what Paul was saying. Paul noticed the man's faith and told him in a loud voice, "Stand up!" The man jumped to his feet and started walking! The people were amazed and said, "These men are gods in human bodies!" "Stop!" cried Paul. "We are only people, just like you. We have come to tell you about the one real God, who made everything. We want to give you the good news that Jesus is God's Son!"

NOVEMBER 30

PAUL AND Barnabas were away on a long trip for several years. Sometimes they walked. Other times they traveled by boat. Wherever they went, they told everyone about Jesus. Many people who listened to them believed in Jesus. Soon there were lots of new churches. When Paul and Barnabas returned to Antioch, Paul worried about the Christians they had left behind. He

wanted to go back to see them and then travel on to preach to more people. Paul and Barnabas knew they needed a helper. But Paul didn't want to take Mark, who had gone with them before and then left them. So the men went to different places, each with his own helper. Barnabas took Mark and sailed to Cyprus. Paul chose Silas to go with him.

DECEMBER 1

PAUL TOOK SILAS to many of the churches that had been started on Paul's first trip. In the town of Lystra, they met a young believer named Timothy. Everyone liked Timothy, so Paul wanted the young man to go with him and Silas on their trip.

Together the three men helped new churches grow strong in faith, and many more people believed in Jesus.

DECEMBER 2

PAUL AND SILAS didn't know ahead of time what town they would visit next. But the Holy Spirit always let them know where God wanted them to go.

When they came to the city of Troas, Paul had a strange dream. In the dream a man from Macedonia was begging him, "Come over here and help us."

Paul knew at once that God wanted him to share the good news about Jesus with the people there. So Paul set off with Silas, sailing across the sea toward Macedonia.

DECEMBER 3

WHEN PAUL AND SILAS arrived in Macedonia, they went to the city of Philippi. At the riverbank, they met a group of women. Paul began talking to them about Jesus. One of the women, Lydia, believed in God. But she hadn't heard about Jesus until she listened to Paul. She and everyone from her house were baptized. Lydia invited Paul and his friends to stay at her house while they were in the city.

DECEMBER 4

PAUL AND SILAS met a slave girl who made lots of money for her masters. Because she had an evil spirit, she could tell people what was going to happen in the future. Paul ordered the evil spirit to come out of her, and it left right away. When the girl's owners saw that she could no longer earn money for them, they had Paul and Silas beaten up and thrown into jail.

That night Paul and Silas sang songs to God even though they were in chains. Suddenly there was a huge earthquake. Every prisoner's chains fell off and all the doors flew open!

DECEMBER 5

WHEN THE JAILER woke up, he was afraid. He thought all the prisoners had escaped. He knew he would be in big trouble. As he pulled out a sword to kill himself, Paul shouted, "Don't hurt yourself. We are all here!" The jailer ran over to Paul and Silas. He asked, "How can I be saved?" Paul told the man about Jesus, and he believed! He took Paul and Silas back to his home. Soon his family believed in Jesus too! The next day, the city leaders told Paul and Silas they were sorry for the way they were treated. Then they told Paul and Silas they were free to go.

DECEMBER 6

PAUL AND SILAS went to Thessalonica next. There Paul visited the Jewish synagogue and told the people all about Jesus. Some of the Jews believed what Paul said. Many Greek people believed too. But some of the Jewish leaders didn't want people listening to Paul and Silas. These leaders got an angry crowd together. They said Paul and Silas were causing trouble all over the world. The believers sent Paul and Silas to another town so the angry crowd couldn't find them. Instead the crowd dragged some other believers to the city leaders. But the city leaders let them go after they paid a fee.

DECEMBER 7

WHEN PAUL WENT to new places, he never forgot the believers that he left behind. After Paul left the believers in Thessalonica, he wrote two letters to them. Paul wrote, "Jesus will come back from heaven. Everyone will hear the sound of God's trumpet. Then all Christians will go up in the clouds to be with Jesus forever!" He also wrote, "Before Jesus comes back, there will be hard times. Many people will turn against Jesus. But God will be with you and give you his peace, no matter what happens."

351

DECEMBER 8

DURING ALL THE trouble in Thessalonica, Paul and Silas left in the middle of the night and went to the town of Berea. The people there wanted to hear Paul's preaching. They read God's Word to learn if what Paul and Silas told them was true. Many Jews and many Greeks believed in Jesus. But when the Jewish leaders in Thessalonica heard about this, they came to Berea. They turned the people against Paul and Silas there too. Again Paul had to leave quickly. He went to Athens, a place near the sea, and told Silas and Timothy to come as soon as they could.

DECEMBER 9

WHILE PAUL WAS IN Athens, he was sad to see how many different gods the people worshiped. But the people who lived in Athens liked to think and to talk. So Paul spoke every day at an outdoor meeting in the city. He said, "I see you've been worshiping a god you call 'The God No One Knows.' I do know him. He's the real God. No human can make a god. God made this world and everything in it. He brought Jesus, his Son, back to life. Jesus will judge the world." Some people laughed. Some wanted to hear more. And others believed Paul's message.

DECEMBER 10

PAUL LEFT ATHENS and went to Corinth. Soon Silas and Timothy joined him. With their help, Paul spent all his time teaching about Jesus. But here too, some of the Jews didn't like what he said. They were mean to him and insulted him. So Paul said he'd preach only to people who wanted to learn about Jesus. God spoke to Paul in a dream. "Don't be afraid! Speak out! I am with you, so no one will be able to hurt you," God said. So Paul stayed in Corinth for a year and a half, teaching the Word of God.

December 11

In Corinth, Paul became good friends with Priscilla and Aquila, a Jewish couple from Italy. Paul lived and worked with them, because they made tents, just like Paul.

When Paul lived with Priscilla and Aquila, he taught them a lot about Jesus. When he left the city, Paul took his new friends with him. They sailed to Ephesus, and from there Paul left to visit many different places. Priscilla and Aquila were able to teach the people in Ephesus everything they had learned about Jesus from Paul.

DECEMBER 12

PRISCILLA AND AQUILA told a man named Apollos about Jesus. Then Apollos was ready to tell everyone the Good News.

He sailed to Achaia to visit the new believers there. Apollos was a big help to them because he was able to help the Jews understand that Jesus was God's promised Savior.

DECEMBER 13

PAUL RETURNED to Ephesus to preach. He did many miracles and helped many people to believe in Jesus. Most of the people worshiped the Greek goddess Diana. They bought silver statues of Diana to keep in their homes. But the new believers didn't worship other gods anymore. Now the men who made the statues weren't selling as many of them. This made them angry. "We need to get rid of this troublemaker!" they said. Soon an angry crowd was looking for Paul to attack him. The mayor of Ephesus finally put a stop to the riot and sent everyone home. Paul was safe!

DECEMBER 14

NOT LONG AFTER the trouble in Ephesus, Paul left the city. He went to the town of Troas and met with the believers on Sunday in an upstairs room. Since he was leaving the next day, Paul preached until midnight. A young man named Eutychus was sitting on a windowsill, where he fell asleep. He fell out of the open window to the ground below and died. But Paul took him in his arms and said, "Don't worry, he's alive!" So the people went back upstairs to eat. And Paul preached until morning came. Meanwhile, someone took Eutychus home. It was amazing—he wasn't even hurt!

DECEMBER 15

PAUL WAS IN A HURRY to go to Jerusalem. Paul and his friends first sailed to a place near Ephesus. Paul sent a message to the church leaders there, asking them to come out to where he was staying. When they arrived, Paul said, "I must go on to Jerusalem. The Holy Spirit has told me that times will be hard there. But I want to do what God wants. None of you will ever see me

again. Take care of God's church in Ephesus." When he finished speaking, Paul prayed with the church leaders. They wept as they hugged Paul good-bye. And they watched sadly as he sailed away.

DECEMBER 16

PAUL STOPPED TO REST at Philip's house. Philip's daughters had the gift of prophecy. They gave people messages from God. While Paul was at Philip's house, a prophet named Agabus visited too. He tied Paul's belt around his own hands and feet. "If you go to Jerusalem, this will happen to you," Agabus told Paul. "Jewish leaders will hand you over to the Romans." Paul's friends begged him not to go, but his mind was made up. "I'm ready not only to be put in jail in Jerusalem, but also to die for the Lord Jesus," he said. And he left, ready to face any danger.

DECEMBER 17

WHEN PAUL CAME to Jerusalem, he went to the temple. Some of his enemies made up a story about him. "This man is teaching people to break God's laws!" they cried. Then they dragged Paul out of the temple. People began to shout and run in all directions. When the leader of the Roman army heard about the angry mob, he hurried to the temple with some of his officers. When they got there, Paul's enemies stopped beating him. The soldiers took Paul to an army building.

The mob followed, shouting, "Kill him! Kill him!" So the soldiers lifted Paul on their shoulders to protect him as they carried him inside the building.

DECEMBER 18

BEFORE THE soldiers took Paul inside the building where he'd be safe, Paul told the army leader that he wanted to talk to the angry crowd. He spoke Greek, a language that the leader understood. So the leader let him stand on the steps and talk. This time Paul spoke in Aramaic, a language the people understood. Paul told them how he came to believe in Jesus. Then Paul said that God wanted him to preach to everyone, not just the Jews. When the crowd heard this, they shouted again, "Kill him!" Then the soldiers quickly took Paul inside.

December 19

THE ARMY LEADER was angry with Paul for getting the crowd upset again. "Take this man and beat him," he told his soldiers. "Maybe then he'll tell us what he's done to upset the Jewish people." As the soldiers began to tie Paul up, he asked, "Isn't it against the law to beat a Roman citizen who may not even have done anything wrong?" Now the soldiers were afraid, so they sent for their leader. "Are you a Roman?" the army leader asked Paul.

"Yes, I am," Paul answered. Then the soldiers stopped their plans to hurt Paul. Even the army leader knew that he had to treat a Roman citizen fairly.

363

DECEMBER 20

THE NEXT DAY the Roman army leader brought Paul to the Jewish leaders. Paul told them he believed God could bring people back to life after they died. Some of the priests agreed with what Paul said, but others didn't. So they began to fight. Some pulled Paul this way, and some pulled him that way. Then soldiers stepped in and took Paul back to the army building. The next morning the Jewish leaders came up with a plan. They decided to ask for another meeting with Paul. Then they would wait for him. When he came out of the building, they would jump out and kill him. They promised each other they wouldn't eat or drink anything until Paul was dead.

DECEMBER 21

PAUL'S NEPHEW HEARD about the Jewish leaders' plan, and he told Paul. So Paul told a soldier to take his nephew to the Roman army leader. "When some Jewish leaders say they want to see Paul again," the nephew said to the army leader, "please don't take him to them. More than 40 men will be waiting to kill him." The army leader believed him. "Don't let anyone know you told me this," he warned. He provided Paul with horses to ride, so he could leave quickly in the middle of the night. And he sent 470 men to go with Paul.

DECEMBER 22

PAUL MADE IT SAFELY out of Jerusalem. He was then taken to Caesarea, a town by the sea. A few days later some of the Jewish leaders talked to Felix, the Roman governor, about Paul.

After listening to Paul tell his story, Felix didn't think Paul had done anything wrong. But he kept Paul in jail because he didn't want to upset the people.

Two years later a new governor named Festus took over. He wanted Paul to return to Jerusalem to be judged in a Jewish court, but Paul refused. Paul wanted to be judged in a Roman court of law, because he was a Roman citizen.

DECEMBER 23

GOVERNOR FESTUS talked to the king about Paul. "He is in jail because he has made some of the Jews so angry that they want him to die. But I don't think Paul has broken any laws."

The next day Paul was brought before the king. Paul told him how he'd become a Christian and how he now spent all his time talking to others about following Jesus. The king agreed with Festus that Paul hadn't done anything wrong. The king said, "If Paul hadn't asked for a Roman trial, you could have set him free. But now he will have to go to Rome."

DECEMBER 24

A ROMAN OFFICER named Julius sailed with Paul to Rome. The trip was long and hard because strong winds kept blowing the ship the wrong way.

At last they stopped at a place called Fair Haven. Since winter was coming, Paul told the officers on the ship, "We should stay here for the winter. It's too dangerous to go on." But the captain wanted to keep going. He sailed the ship right into a terrible storm. For many days, huge waves hit the boat. Everyone was so afraid! They couldn't even see the sun or the stars.

DECEMBER 25

NO ONE ATE a thing for two weeks. Paul was the only one who wasn't afraid. "You should have listened to me!" he said. "Then we wouldn't be in danger. But be brave! Last night an angel told me that God will keep all of us safe." Paul talked everyone into eating. "You need strength to stay alive," he said. The next day the ship hit sand at the bottom of the sea and broke apart. Some of the men swam toward the shore. Those who couldn't swim held on to broken pieces of the boat. Everyone made it safely to shore, just as the angel said!

DECEMBER 26

ONCE EVERYONE WAS SAFE on shore, they learned they were on the island of Malta. The people there were very kind and made a fire to warm the wet, tired group. As Paul was putting wood on the fire, a poisonous snake slid out of the woodpile and began to wind itself around his hand. "This man must be a murderer," the island people said. "God must have sent the snake to kill him even though he lived through the storm." But Paul shook off the snake. It didn't hurt him at all! The people were amazed. They thought Paul was a god.

DECEMBER 27

THE LEADER of Malta, Publius, welcomed the shipwrecked men and let them stay at his house for three days. Publius' father was in bed with a fever. So Paul prayed, and he got well. Others heard about this, and soon everyone on the island who was sick came to Paul to be made well. Paul and the men stayed on Malta for three months. When winter was over, they were ready to go to Rome. So they got ready to sail on another boat. But before they left, the people of Malta made sure Paul and the others had everything they needed for their trip. Finally Paul made it to Rome. There he preached about Jesus and waited for his trial.

DECEMBER 28

AFTER ANOTHER long trip, Paul and the soldiers reached Italy. But there were still many miles to travel on land before they came to the city of Rome. They stayed for a week in a town where they met some of Jesus' followers. Then they began the last part of their trip. Paul was very tired as they got nearer to the city, but a happy surprise was waiting for him. A few people who believed in Jesus were waiting to welcome him and walk with him along the last part of the road. And when Paul finally arrived in Rome, instead of putting him in jail, the Romans let him live in a house. But a soldier stood guard over him.

DECEMBER 29

PAUL WASN'T FREE to leave his house. But anyone could visit him. So Paul invited the Jews who lived in Rome to his house. He told them that Jesus was the Savior they had been waiting for. But, like Jewish people in other cities, some didn't want to listen. So Paul invited the people who weren't Jewish to visit him, and he told them the good news about Jesus. For two years, Paul lived in his own house with a soldier guarding the door. During this time no one stopped him from teaching about Jesus. Paul wrote letters to encourage the growing churches in all the places he had visited.

DECEMBER 30

JOHN, ONE OF JESUS' 12 disciples, was now an old man. The Roman leaders had sent him to live alone on the island of Patmos so he couldn't talk about Jesus. But that didn't stop John from writing to the churches.

As John was praying one day, Jesus himself appeared to John from heaven. His face was bright like the sun, and his voice sounded like a trumpet! He said, "I'll be alive forever! Write to the churches about all that you see and hear. Tell how things are and how they will be."

DECEMBER 31

JOHN SAW BEAUTIFUL pictures of heaven in his mind and wrote down what he saw. "I saw a new heaven and a new earth," he wrote. "God will live with us forever, and he'll wipe away everyone's tears. No one will be sad or have any more pain."

Then an angel showed John a city with streets made of shiny gold. The walls were set with beautiful jewels. This city didn't need the sun and the moon, because Jesus gave the city its light. There was no night, and there was no evil. How wonderful God's kingdom was! And everyone there loved Jesus!

PEOPLE OF THE OLD TESTAMENT

AARON
Moses' brother. He spoke for God when they went to see the king of Egypt.

ABEL
Second son of Adam and Eve. Abel was killed by his jealous brother Cain.

ABRAHAM
Because he trusted and obeyed God, he became the father of the nation of Israel.

ABRAHAM, SARAH, AND ISAAC

ADAM
The first man God created and husband of Eve. They sinned against God and had to leave the Garden of Eden.

CAIN
First son of Adam and Eve. He killed his brother Abel in a jealous rage.

DANIEL
An Israelite who rose to an important position in Babylon. He had a gift for explaining what dreams meant. He was thrown into the lions' den by King Darius.

DAVID
A shepherd boy from Bethlehem who became king of Israel. He was also a great musician.

ELIJAH
A great prophet of Israel. He stood up to King Ahab, a bad king who wanted God's people to worship false gods.

ELISHA
The man who followed Elijah as God's prophet.

ESAU
Jacob's twin brother and the son of Isaac and Rebecca.

ESTHER
The young Jewish queen of King Xerxes. She saved her people from being killed.

EVE

EVE
The first woman God created. She was the first person to disobey God.

EZEKIEL
A prophet in Babylon who warned God's people about the fall of Jerusalem.

GOLIATH
A giant Philistine soldier who challenged the Israelites. He was killed by David.

HAMAN
Chief minister of King Xerxes. He plotted to kill the Jews.

HANNAH
Mother of Samuel.

ISAAC
Son of Abraham and Sarah, husband of Rebecca and father of Esau and Jacob.

ISAIAH
A prophet who told about the coming of the Messiah.

JACOB
Son of Isaac and Rebecca, and younger twin brother of Esau. He stole Esau's blessing.

JEREMIAH
A prophet in Judah who warned that Jerusalem would be destroyed and God's people forced to leave home.

JOB
A man who lost everything he had, but still believed in God.

JONAH
A prophet who didn't obey God. He was swallowed by a big fish.

JONAH

JONATHAN
The son of King Saul. He warned David that his father wanted to kill him.

JOSEPH
Jacob's favorite son. He was sold as a slave in Egypt, where he became powerful. He saved Egypt and his family from starving.

JOSHUA
One of Moses' helpers. He became the leader of God's people after Moses' death.

MOSES

MOSES
A great leader and prophet, who led God's people out of Egypt and then to the Promised Land.

NAOMI
Ruth's mother-in-law.

NEHEMIAH
He helped to rebuild the city of Jerusalem when the Jewish people returned home.

NOAH
God saved him and his family from the great Flood by telling them to build an ark.

RACHEL
Daughter of Laban and wife of Jacob.

REBECCA
Wife of Isaac and mother of Jacob and Esau.

RUTH
Daughter-in-law of Naomi and wife of Boaz.

SAMSON
An Israelite with great strength who fought the Philistines. He lost his strength when the Philistines cut off his hair.

SAMUEL
The prophet who anointed the first kings of Israel, Saul and David.

SARAH
Wife of Abraham and mother of Isaac.

SAUL
The first king of Israel. He later disobeyed God.

SOLOMON
He followed his father David as king of Israel. He built the temple in Jerusalem and was famous for being wise.

ZEDEKIAH
The last king of Judah. He was taken prisoner by the Babylonians. He died in exile far away from home.

PEOPLE OF THE NEW TESTAMENT

ANANIAS
A believer in Damascus who prayed for Paul to be cured of his blindness.

ANDREW
Brother of Peter and one of the 12 disciples.

BARNABAS
A Christian who went with Paul on a missionary journey to Cyprus.

ELIZABETH AND MARY

ELIZABETH
John the Baptist's mother, and Mary's cousin.

GABRIEL
The angel who told Mary she would give birth to Jesus.

HEROD AGRIPPA
Grandson of Herod the Great. Along with Festus, he heard the Jewish leaders' case against Paul

HEROD ANTIPAS
Son of Herod the Great. He gave the order for John the Baptist to be beheaded.

HEROD THE GREAT
King of Judah when Jesus was born. He gave an order for all the baby boys in Bethlehem to be killed.

JAMES
One of the 12 disciples. He was John's brother and a close friend of Jesus.

JESUS
The Son of God, who came to earth and died to save everyone from their sins.

JOHN THE APOSTLE
One of the 12 disciples and brother of James.
He was a close friend of Jesus.

JOHN THE BAPTIST
Son of Zechariah and Elizabeth. He was sent by God to prepare people for the coming of the Messiah. He was beheaded by Herod Antipas.

JOSEPH
A carpenter from Nazareth who married Mary, the mother of Jesus.

JOSEPH OF ARIMATHEA
The man who provided a tomb for Jesus' body.

JUDAS ISCARIOT
One of the twelve disciples. He betrayed Jesus.

LAZARUS
A friend of Jesus and brother of Mary and Martha. Jesus raised him from the dead.

MARTHA
Sister of Mary and Lazarus. A good friend of Jesus.

MARY
The mother of Jesus and wife of Joseph the carpenter.

JOSEPH, MARY, AND JESUS

MARY MAGDALENE
A devoted follower of Jesus. She was the first person to see Jesus after he had risen from the dead.

MARY OF BETHANY
Sister of Martha and Lazarus and a good friend of Jesus. She poured expensive perfume over Jesus' feet.

MATTHEW
A tax collector who became one of the twelve disciples.

PAUL
An enemy of the early church who was converted on the road to Damascus. He became the church's first missionary.

PAUL

PETER
Brother of Andrew, he was one of the 12 disciples. He became a leader among the first Christians in Jerusalem.

PHILIP THE APOSTLE
One of the 12 disciples.

PHILIP THE EVANGELIST
One of the seven helpers. He performed many miracles.

PONTIUS PILATE

PONTIUS PILATE
Roman governor who gave the order for Jesus to be crucified, even though he believed him to be innocent.

SALOME
Daughter of Herodias who asked Herod Antipas for the head of John the Baptist on a plate.

SILAS
A leader of the early Church. He traveled with Paul on some of his missionary journeys.

SIMON
One of the 12 disciples.

SIMON THE MAGICIAN
A man from Samaria who tried to buy the power of the Holy Spirit from Peter and John.

STEPHEN
One of the first leaders of the early Church. He was the first Christian to be killed for his beliefs.

THOMAS
One of the twelve disciples. He doubted that Jesus had risen from the dead until he saw Jesus' wounds for himself.

TIMOTHY
A young man who joined Paul on some of his missionary journeys.

ZECHARIAH
Father of John the Baptist and husband of Elizabeth. He was a priest at the temple in Jerusalem.

ZECHARIAH

INDEX

"For I know the plans I have for you," says the Lord.
"They are plans for good and not for disaster,
to give you a future and a hope."

JEREMIAH 29:11